The Secret of Livermore

"Analyzing the Livermore Market Key System"

Published by Murine Press

The Secret of Livermore

"Analyzing the Market Key System"

By Andras M. Nagy

Murine Press

Other Titles by Andras Nagy

Please check our website for more titles

www.andras-nagy.com

www.spread-traders.com

Dedication

To my daughter Dora

Table of Contents

Acknowledgements

"Give a man a fish; you have fed him for today. Teach a man to fish; and you have fed him for a lifetime. Teach a man to sell fish and he eats steak."—Author unknown

I like to thank to the traders I ran across during my career. Many authors were influential to my trading but no one left a mark on me like reading the fictional life Story of Jesse Livermore - *The Reminiscence of a Stock Operator.*

Reading is very important about trading but only experience and actual practicing can amount to a real value that you can lean on. I always made an attempt to talk and get a feel for traders their psychology in order to learn this craft. I like to thank Robert (Bobby) Kern in Chicago to allow countless telephone and in person dialogues to exchange ideas to see where individual futures may go.

I have met Bobby while I was looking for a clearing firm at the Board of Trade; unfortunately he was closing their clearing business due to personal tragedy of illness and death in the Kern family.

Even after I left Chicago we kept in touch for many years via the phone and always talked about the world markets. He traded family and clients money without live quotes and expensive quote machines. Despite my technology background I had to learn to keep trading simple and low overhead. Many great traders and money managers of course had the same approach as I learned later.

Preface

The majority of men meet with failure because of their lack of persistence in creating new plans to take the place of those, which fail.

- Napoleon Hill

Would you like to know the failure rate for new businesses in general?

It's really high, even in-- maybe especially in-- such can't fail businesses as restaurants and taverns. Some of it has as much as a 90% failure rate and that without any illegal shenanigans are being pulled by anybody. But, people still keep starting businesses, and some still manage to succeed in spite of all the minefields placed against them.

Nobody ever built a successful business by quitting the first time they take a few lumps.

Many traders had experiences with the markets and later after much soul searching they realize the mistakes they made prior and want to try again. Markets of course change in subtle ways.

Who is this book written for?

This book is for anyone who is fascinated with Livermore and his legend and wants to learn what made him successful.

How to use this book

This book works with code and software. The reader will see how each piece fits in and forms complete and comprehensive analysis of the Livermore System. It is meant to serve as a basis to develop a robust trading system using the swing and long term trading mechanics of the system that made Livermore a millionaire 4 times before he finally tired out and gave up.

The reader can either get the one of the software packages or type it in from the book or he can email the author and he will make it available.

There are huge problems with TradeStation and Wealth-lab. They are namely referring price bars in the past and having any manipulation and logic impacted on them. Any 'canned' software you could run into the similar hardship and do not even know that the results are false and unpredictable.

I have the source code for a multi portfolio based test harness and I make that available to convert and develop *Market Key* based trading software.

As I have stated before I don't suggest anyone use the trade station code as a turnkey trading system. It is not ready. It is the code and base interpretation of Livermore, as I understand it.

Introduction

Background

Speculative Markets have a long history. Rice futures have been traded in Japan as early as 17th century, the oldest *known* futures market. There is some evidence that the Chinese traded rice futures as early as 6000 years ago.

The need of futures stemmed from the problems of maintaining a supply of seasonal and storable commodities such as agricultural products and livestock.

With the advent of industrial age industrial and transportation companies were formed and public share ownership was introduced. With this advent the modern day stock market was formed on the curb

Trading and leverage

In the days of Livermore the stocks could be purchased on a 10-percent margin and spread betting like bucket shops were legal in the United States as well.

This leverage is a double edge sword however. Due to volatility of price movements the margin amount can evaporate. If the margin is 5% and the commodity contract held experiences and adverse price movement of 2 percent you have just lost 40 percent of your margin money.

Conversely if you have a favorable trade and experience a move of 5 percent in your favor then you had a 100% returns on your money.

It is clear why commodity markets bring out fear and greed in people. Large traders of commodity futures own baseball teams and enjoy the freedoms and independence not afforded to most people. To simply put it - "the possibilities are horrendous but the downside is equally severe."

If you think it over this is nature's law. It is hard to come by an opportunity sweet without some inherent costs and risks. I will teach you how to cope with the risks by managing it and accept is as part of life. Trading is a business and futures traders have it made once they are profitable and consistent. It is an ideal business, trading is.

Ideal for several reasons;

1) No need for customers
2) Relatively low overhead
3) Expand by multiplying the contracts you buy

Let's look at these points in detail, shall we?

Customers what customers?

The biggest hurdle of any new venture is to gain a basic group of followers and establish clientele. Massive advertising and giveaways are designed to do just that. Some ventures seem easy to start only to realize that your competition is massive and they can buy and sell you multiple times over. How do you compete with such a group of competitors? Well You can start by distinguishing yourself from the group and offer exceptional service. Even if you do the best job you can muster your competition will claim to be better whether it is true or not. I do not wish to elaborate on this further but we can all agree on the competitive nature of business. There is even a book called "Swim with the Sharks".

A real beauty of any trading business **NEEDS NO CUSTOMERS**!

Relative low overhead

A trading business is not a huge overhead if done properly. Consider that a McDonald franchise is more than a million dollars and many other franchise and service ventures are quite expensive we can safely say – entry to trading can be done on a shoestring.

You can even trade while keep a day job. You can't do it with many other businesses since study shows that small business owner virtually work all the time.

Expansion is with push of a button

Robert Kanter the ex-president of ETG who taught me the fine art of exchange listed trading. He used to tell rookies to trade 50 shares of stocks and sometimes even less. Once profitable he said you could expand your business by adding a zero. Consider that other businesses must go though market analysis and borrow money to expand this seems easy in comparison.

The risk of failure in trading is no different from opening a restaurant or a business venue. Statistics show that the odds are roughly equal. Upfront investments can differ of course. In trading sooner you are on the right track lower is your "tuition" to enter into the trading business. I congratulate you on buying this course and investing a little in order perhaps to save a lot more.

There are other advantages of futures versus buy and hold and stock market investing. Namely one is the unbiased market direction.
As you perhaps know or heard that the stock markets have historical upward bias namely caused by inflation and other considerations (such as politics)
No such thing exists in the futures markets. The commodity markets are not upward bias and can and do go down as easy as up. Taking positions in the falling market is what futures traders call short position.
Going short in stock required the up tick rule. In addition since stocks need to be 'borrowed' to be used as shorts not all firm has equal access to this "short list" this hindered many 'bears' and forced them to trade options or use expensive strategies called 'bullets'.

This terminology is the same in the stock markets and futures. The easy of going short pales in comparison the hardships and pain to go short in stocks – it will depend on your broker. The average retail customer has no chance to execute shorts and conventional wisdom and sometimes stupidity frowns of shorts as doomsayers and Un-American. This is the misinformation permeated from Wall Street.

Imagine a casino that has the edge in all forms of betting activity. Would this Casino tell their customers the proper ways of gaming? Well the proper ways of gaming would be **NOT PLAYING** *or* limiting you to the few activities that can yield profits. Card Counting and Poker are the two. No in the millions years – Casinos would ban card counting and often do not even offer poker even so they can make modest profits from it.

The situation is no different from Wall Street. Dumber the average player remains better off the inside players can do. Do not look from meaningful and informative comments from Wall Street insiders and that includes Media, Wall Street Journal.

I am not saying that there is some conspiracy or collusion out there. Simply said – much what is coming from the corner – "buy and hold is good", "mutual funds are the Holy Grail", "futures are inherently more dangerous than stocks" are all nonsense yet they were all invented and permeated to confuse and keep the average folk in the dark.

Real life shows that "buy and hold" can put you in the poorhouse, Mutual fund can rip off and overcharge the public, and stock trading can lose the greenback the same way as futures trading. The latest buzz is day trading. It is a great money machine to clearing firms, "Big Brokers" and their LLP partners.

Yes, you can make money in day trading and by all means try it if that is what you want. But watch out for anything that is promoted and pushed too much in the mainstream. It is often done with a false pretense.

Do not let this stop you from following your dreams. Trade the way your heart desires and follow your dream but do it with one foot at least on earn firmly grounded while you reach for the sky.
Practically everything that's been written during the past fifty years has been a restatement of Livermore and Wyckoff. One of the most important lessons I learned from all three was to trade what you see, not what you think.

Chapter 1

Basic Information

Before Mastery - Chop Wood Carry Water
After Mastery - Chop Wood Carry Water
Anonymous Zen Master

Speculative markets can be described as continuous auction markets and as clearinghouses for the latest supply and demand information.

The meeting places of buyers and sellers, the Stocks and Futures market today include an ever-expanding list of commodities such as: agricultural products, metals, petroleum, and financial instruments, foreign currencies and stock indexes not to mention ~6000 common stocks.

Interesting fact is that major patterns in the market do no change. This is mainly driven by the human element of fear and greed. The techniques Jesse Livermore used to analyze the stock market is as valid as ever. The trend following concepts and swing trading ideas of his market system is also valid today.

The basis of the Livermore system bears similarity to the wave theory. (I never studied or gotten too much into Elliot's school of thought due to my laziness. The similarities are actually superficial.

How to Trade In Stocks

How to Trade in Stocks was copyrighted in 1940 - the year Livermore died. It is believed that he wrote the book in a desperate attempt to raise capital.

The book talks about the rationale of Livermore's decision-making process while trading.

Its ten chapters are:

I.   The Challenge of Speculation

II.   When Does a Stock Act Right?

III.   Follow the Leaders

IV.   Money in the Hand

V.   The Pivotal Point

VI.   The Million-Dollar Blunder

VII.   The Three Million Dollar Profit

VIII.   The Livermore Market Key

IX.   Explanatory Rules

X.   Charts and Explanations for the Livermore Market Key

In this book we focus on the inherent logic and code of the system. Many earlier issues chapter IX and X are missing due to some unscrupulous characters whom tried to keep secrets from the general public. Even when these chapters are present the full understanding of Livermore's system one needs detective work and some amount of speculating to grasp the meaning of the Market Key.

I believe in no secrets when it concerns a public domain subject that is so huge and so important. I can't understand how someone believed that the truth could be suppressed.

Livermore places the markets in certain states;

- Up Trend

- Natural Rally

- Secondary Rally

- Down Trend

- Natural Reaction

- Secondary Reaction

The system also determines a number of pivot points as defined by Livermore, the names of the corresponding variables used in the program are in parenthesis

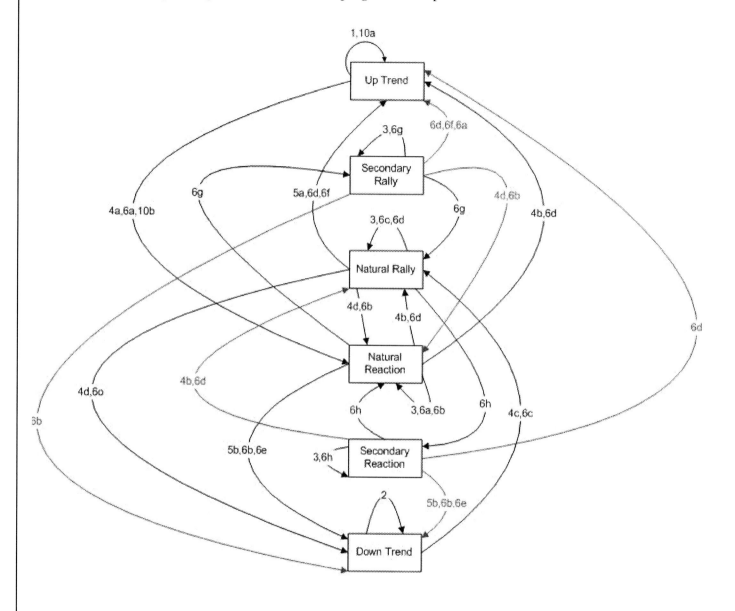

The above figure measures the state of each bar using the values recommended by Livermore

The following figure depicts the state of each bar using an ATR threshold.

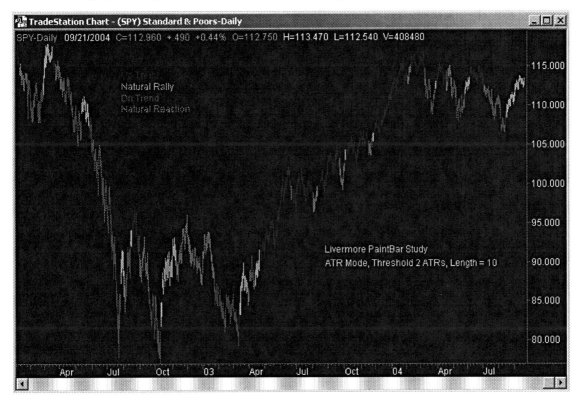

The states "Natural Rally" and "Natural Reaction" are inherent corrections to bull markets. Livermore states in his writing that a reaction in a bull market is welcome and natural as breathing fresh air. It does several key things;

If it is early enough it lets in latecomers to the market who for some reason had missed the rally. It 'sorts out' the weak hands from the strong hands. Many impatient and undercapitalized traders get out too soon only to panic and return later only to further fuel the rally.

The market needs to settle and get ready for the continuation if that is to come.

The limitations of the Livermore system as is

As to this day I am testing and found only the 6 points and percentage (non-original setting) working with the stock market. Futures testing (on S&P ten-year data) so far proved to be losers. The fixed six-point setting is fine when the stock price above 30. I am testing with historical data that has lower prices (as early as 1988) and a dynamic percentage method is best.

In Livermore's days stock operators worked on a 10-percent margin. So when Livermore states 6-points threshold in his book for a 30-dollar stock he is referring a 20-percent pullback. Think in terms of $3 = 1 margin, $6 two-margins and $12=4-margins when computing the threshold.

The book Livermore wrote explains the market turns as a formation of a pattern double top or double bottom. This is not part of the code and there was no logic to account for this rule. It is obvious that one can't discount a market turn in a V shape (as it happens) but one must make provisions for a failsafe rule.

(Much like the turtle system false break out rule)

On page 44 Livermore discusses the "pivotal point".

"For example: Take a stock, which has been in a Downward Trend for sometime and reaches a low point at 40. Then it has a quick rally in a few days to 45, then it backs and fills for a week in a range of a few points, and then it starts to extend its rally until it reaches 49 ½.

The market becomes dull and inactive for a few days. Then one day it becomes active again and foes down 3-4 points, and keeps going down until it reaches near the pivotal point near 40."

I am still pondering this and the puzzle it presents to code the system into a concrete set of rules. Ideally the fail-safe rule will be an option and one can test multitudes of scenarios with and with out it. This I leave for the application development but continue with testing in Wealth-lab.

The Key price using the aggregate price of the leader and the follower is not used in my model simply because to software limitations.

Livermore used to follow 2-3 prices when followed a sector. If he traded steel stocks he would follow US Steel and Bethlehem Steel. One was always the leader if the group and the other were the laggard. He would also add the prices together and use them as the key price. The threshold used for the key price was double of the threshold used for individual stocks. The reason for this was to get a confirmation of the move from the laggard. If the laggard showed a pivotal point he could be more assured that the signal in the leader will make him money.

Livermore tried to get an edge on his competitors anyway he could get.

Using the Key Price is not yet part of my code in either back-testing platform mainly due to programming difficulties and trying to keep the scripts clean and understandable

Translation to Wealth-lab developer

TradeStation 2000i while may be a very widely used platform is not my favorite. I do not like the programming language or the interface. I am transforming the code into Wealth-lab developer or try using it manually with Track N Trade Pro 4.0 – my favorite charting package. Ideally if you are a programmer you should just bite the bullet and code up a testing or trading harness in C++ or some other flexible and useful PC programming language. We have access to offshore teams and have done at least a hundred small projects ranging from $100 to $1500.

This code and book is not a turnkey system to get rich with. This is an educational and research project to better us as traders and honor Livermore as well.

There are programmatic limitations in all packaged software like TS 2000I and Wealth-lab. Copies you may purchase will end up in the mothball for lack of support and enhancement from the company due to nefarious dealings with broker firms.

Coding strategies may result in unpredictable results like in TradeStation referring to a bar back several days or even weeks may prove to be problematic at best. It all seems to work but in reality it does not.

The DIS chart below shows the system's forte in picking out trends.

In this instance the Yellow (Natural Reaction State) is rather short and we get out on the top. The reader may want to get out during the natural Reaction State when long and this state has a severe draw-dawn.

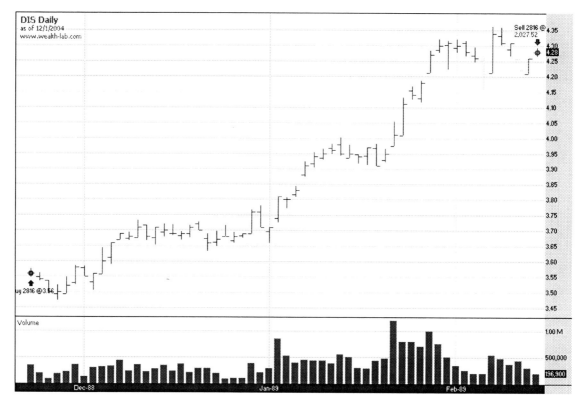

The second chart shows that the Natural Reaction can be more severe. It is possible to get out and reenter the trade when the up trend resumes. Right now the system is not programmed that way.

Flowchart of Livermore's Secret

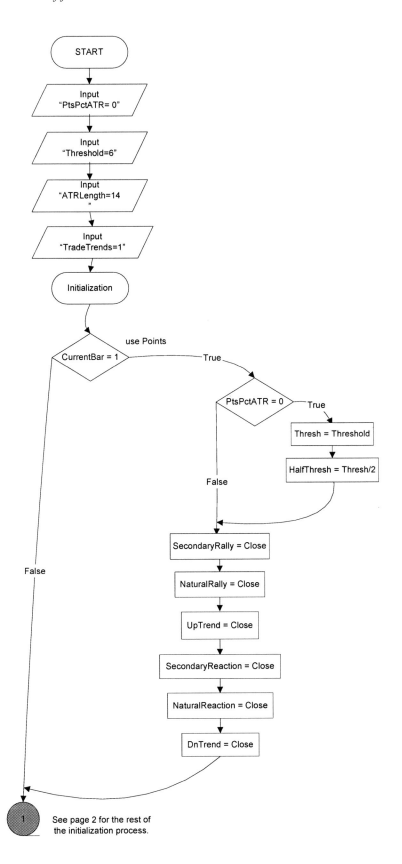

START

Input
"PtsPctATR= 0"

Input
"Threshold=6"

Input
"ATRLength=14
"

Input
"TradeTrends=1"

Initialization

CurrentBar = 1

use Points

True

False

PtsPctATR = 0

True

False

Thresh = Threshold

HalfThresh = Thresh/2

SecondaryRally = Close

NaturalRally = Close

UpTrend = Close

SecondaryReaction = Close

NaturalReaction = Close

DnTrend = Close

1

See page 2 for the rest of
the initialization process.

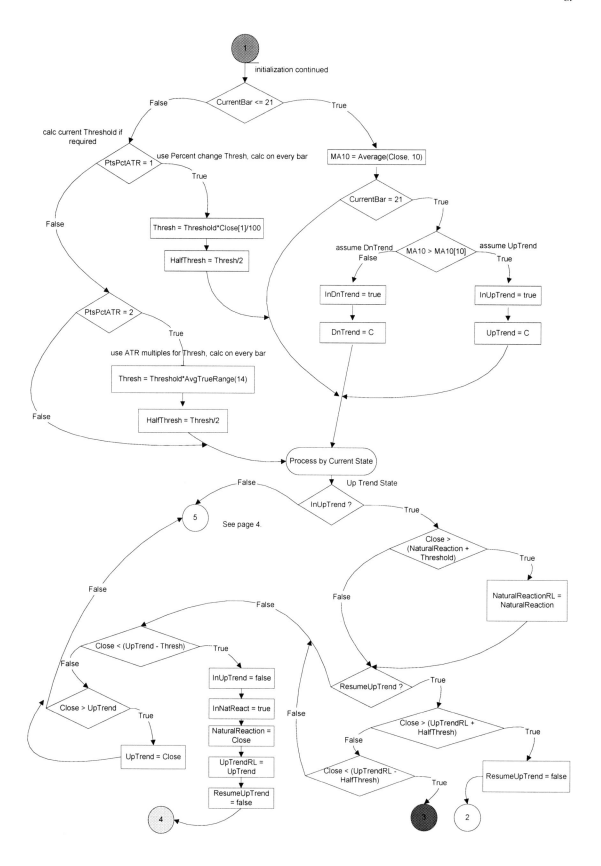

1

initialization continued

CurrentBar <= 21

False / True

calc current Threshold if required

PtsPctATR = 1 — use Percent change Thresh, calc on every bar

True

Thresh = Threshold*Close[1]/100

HalfThresh = Thresh/2

False

PtsPctATR = 2

True

use ATR multiples for Thresh, calc on every bar

Thresh = Threshold*AvgTrueRange(14)

HalfThresh = Thresh/2

False

MA10 = Average(Close, 10)

CurrentBar = 21

True

assume DnTrend   MA10 > MA10[10]   assume UpTrend
False   True

InDnTrend = true   InUpTrend = true

DnTrend = C   UpTrend = C

Process by Current State

Up Trend State

InUpTrend ?

False / True

5

See page 4.

Close > (NaturalReaction + Threshold)

True

NaturalReactionRL = NaturalReaction

False

False

Close < (UpTrend - Thresh)

True

InUpTrend = false

InNatReact = true

NaturalReaction = Close

UpTrendRL = UpTrend

ResumeUpTrend = false

False

Close > UpTrend

True

UpTrend = Close

4

ResumeUpTrend ?

True

Close > (UpTrendRL + HalfThresh)

False / True

Close < (UpTrendRL - HalfThresh)

False

True

ResumeUpTrend = false

3

2

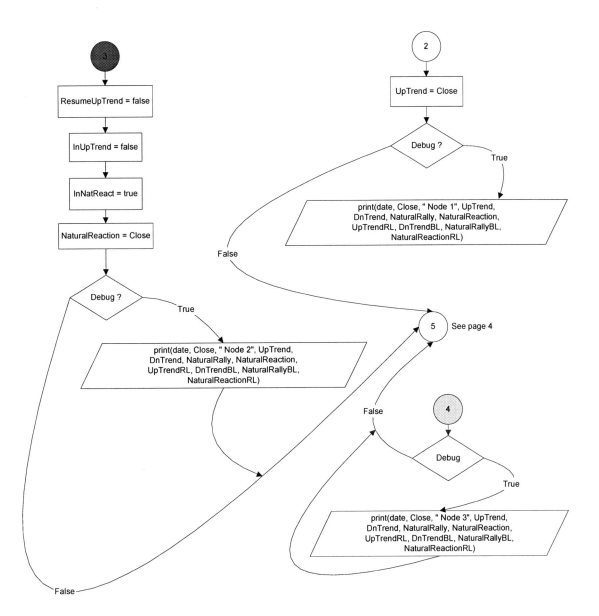

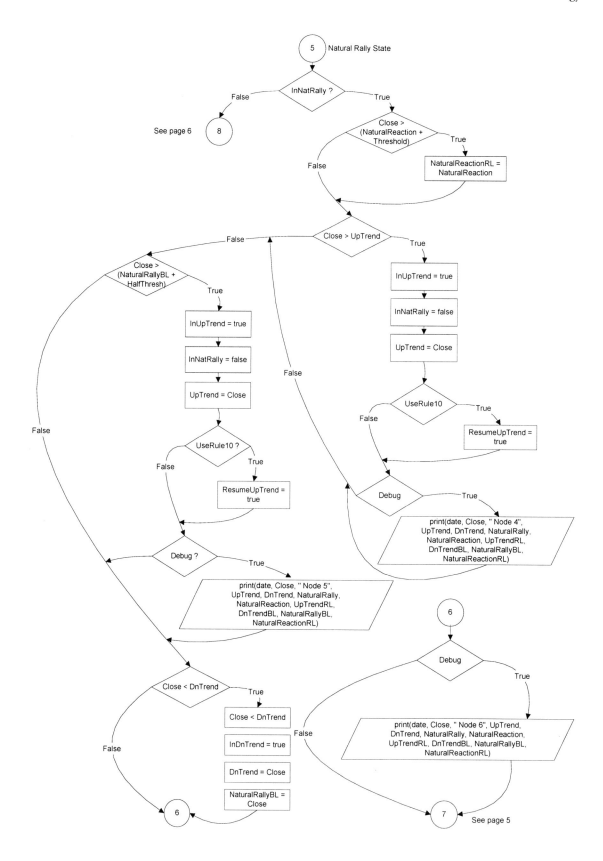

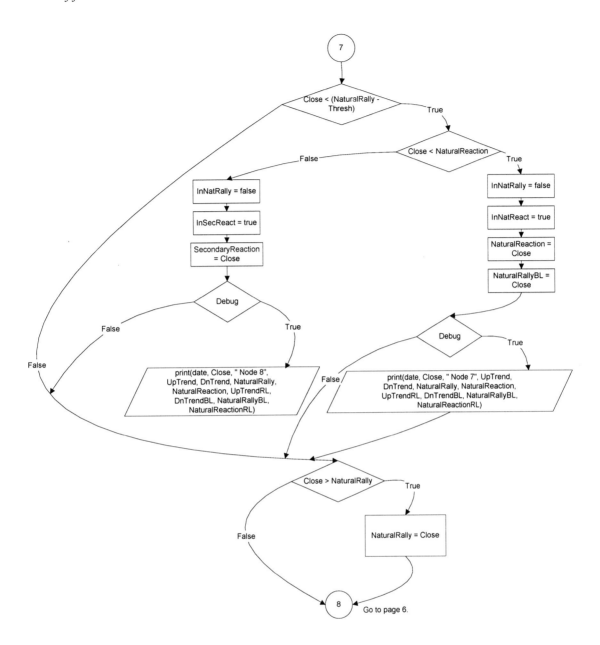

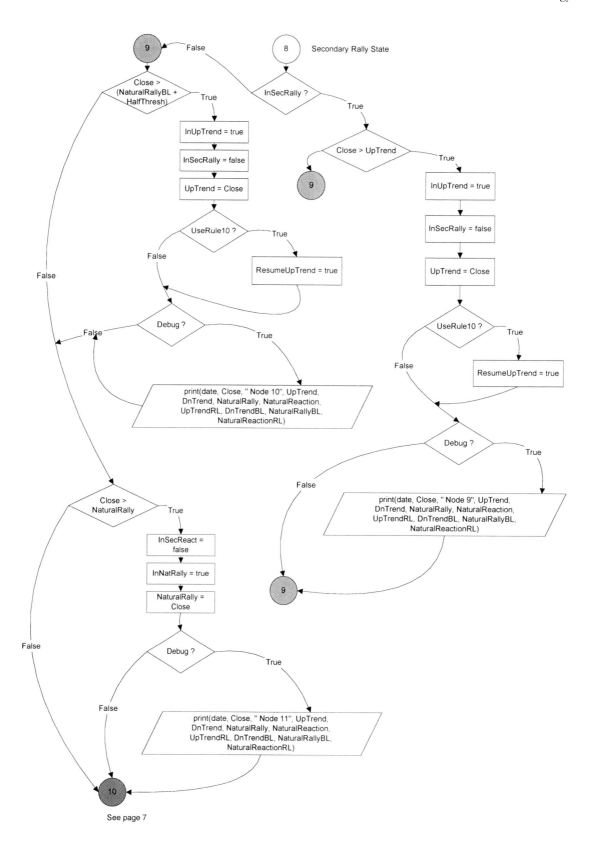

See page 7

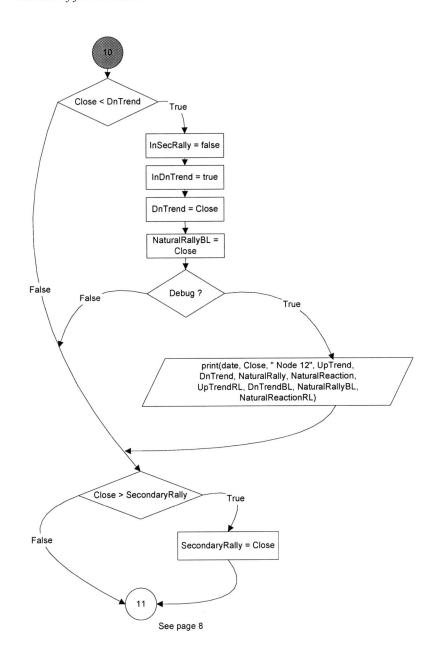

See page 8

34

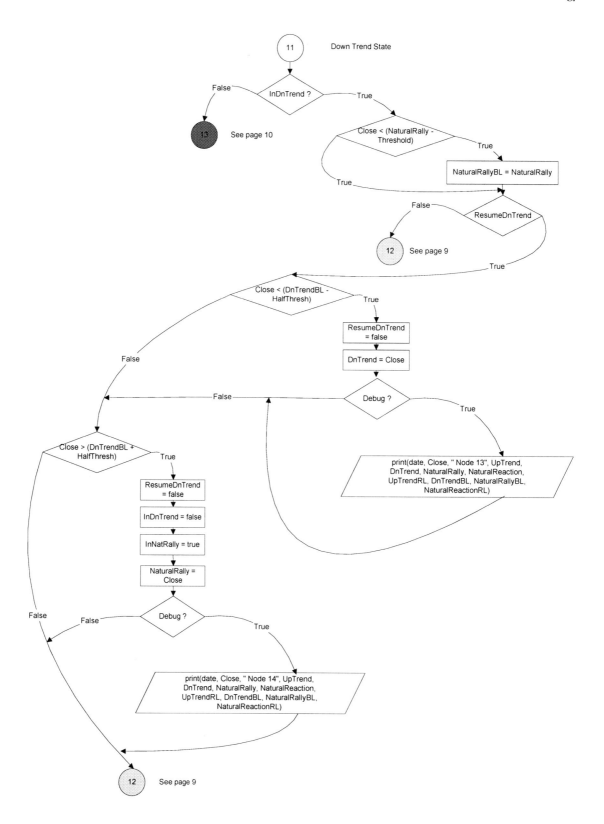

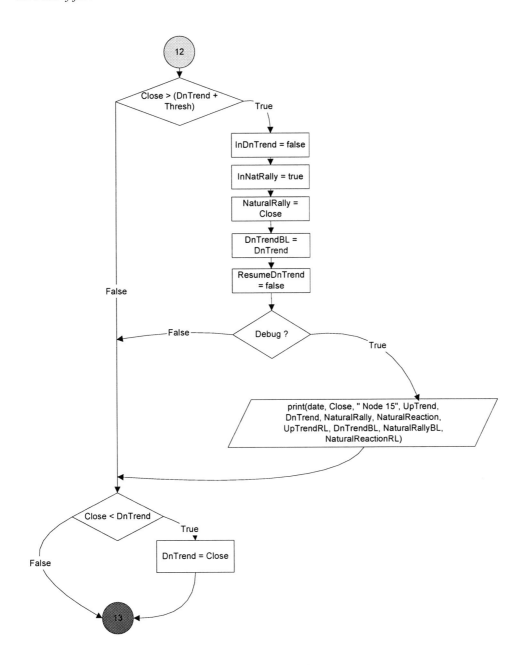

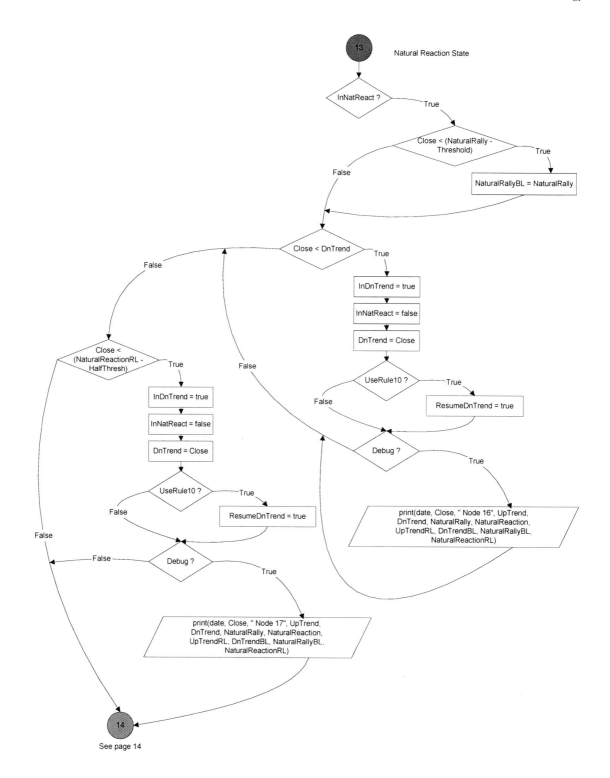

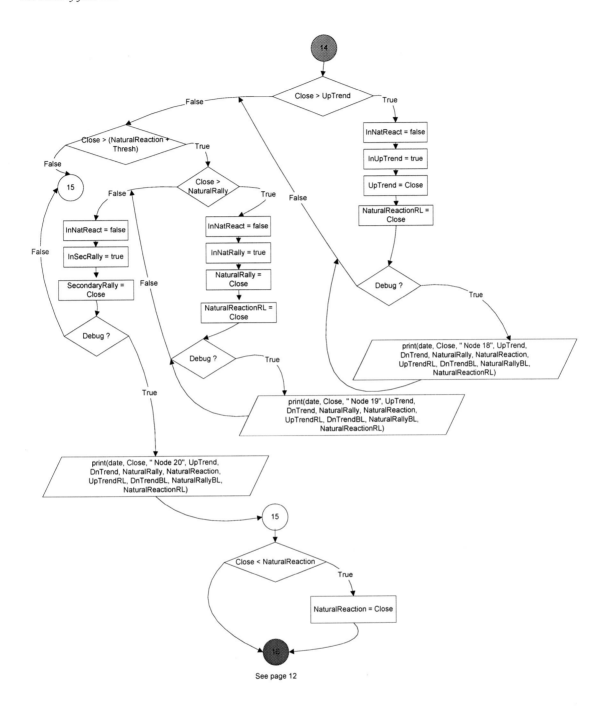

See page 12

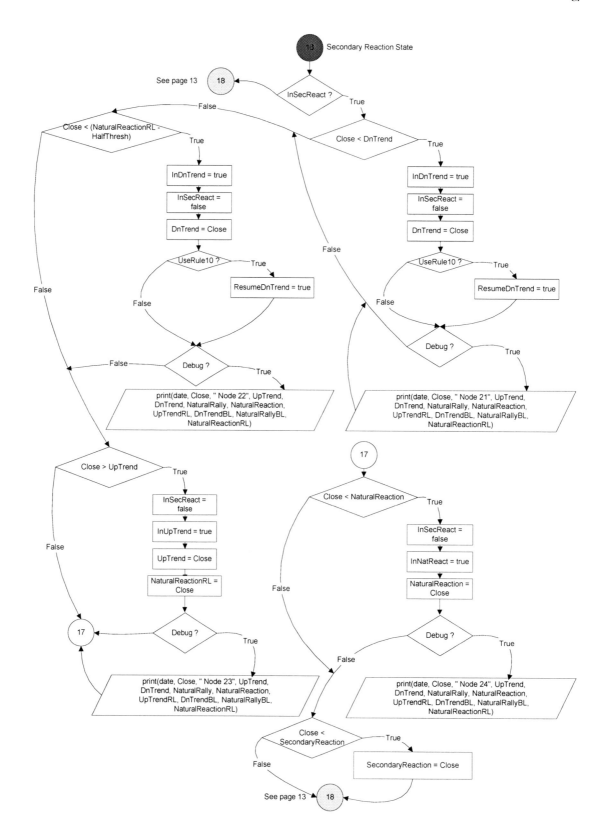

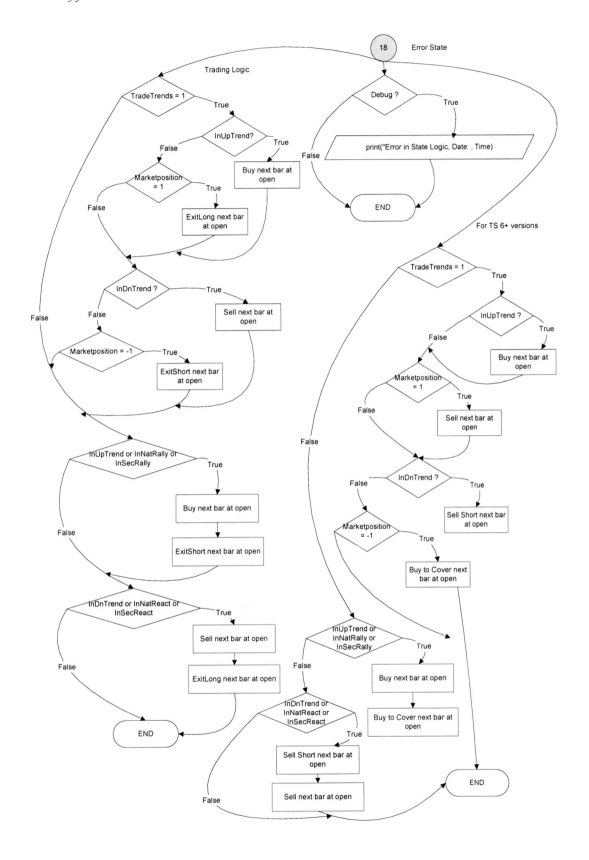

Explaining the Rules

The first step in the Livermore system is to identify the current state of the market. According to Livermore there could be six states but initially we make a determination to place us in either in a downtrend or an up-trend. We do not attempt to figure out the market's state at the finer granularity.

We determine the trend by using the 10-day moving average on the 21st day and compare it to the 10-day moving average from 10 days ago. This is only one way of doing it and I can think of several methods that can be used and tested.

The system of Livermore is essentially managing and examining the states the market is in.

    Up Trend

    Down Trend

    Natural Rally

    Secondary Rally

    Natural Reaction

    Secondary Reaction

But as we said initially we are either in up-trend or downtrend.

We also have to initialize some variables like: (think of these as the blank columns on Livermore's charts)

    Secondary Rally equals today's Closing Price;

    Natural Rally equals today's Closing Price;

    Up Trend equals today's Closing Price;

    Secondary Reaction equals today's Closing Price;

    Natural Reaction equals today's Closing Price;

    Down Trend equals today's Closing Price;

    Threshold equals 10-percent;

Placeholders such as NaturalRallyBL, NaturalReactionRL, UpTrendRL, and DnTrendBL are for the *color marker* rules Livermore was so fond of. BL = Black Line RL= Red Line

Most price comparison is a setup to change the state or record price information.

When we are in up trend

Whenever in other states we qualify to Up Trend State we come here

If the today's Closing Price is greater than the NaturalReaction plus the Threshold then

Record new price:

NaturalReactionRL equals NaturalReaction; {Rule 4b}

If we adhere to rule 10 rule[1] then check if ResumeUpTrend equals with true

{Rule 10 logic.}

We must look at;

If the today's Closing Price is greater than UpTrendRL plus Half the Threshold value then

(UpTrendRL is up-trend price market by red line 10a)

We must change the state to natural reaction and record that price (see below)

NaturalReaction equals today's Closing Price;

UpTrend equals today's Closing Price;

If the today's Closing Price is less then the UpTrendRL[2] minus HalfThreshold then

We must change the state to natural reaction and record that price (see below)

ResumeUpTrend equals false; {Rule 10b}

{We change the state to natural reaction}

NaturalReaction equals today's Closing Price

End of rule 10 logic

If today's Closing Price is less than UpTrend minus Threshold then {start NaturalReaction}

{Rules 4a, 6a}

{We change the state to natural reaction}

Record the following new prices;

UpTrendRL[3] equals UpTrend; {pivot point, rule 8}

NaturalReaction equals today's Closing Price;

ResumeUpTrend equals false;

If today's Closing Price is greater than UpTrend then {remain in up-trend higher high price}

---

[1] Rule 10 is optional and require further testing
[2] Last up-trend price marked with Red Line (RL)

Record the following new prices;

UpTrend equals today's Closing Price;

End {InUpTrend}

When we are in Natural Rally State

Whenever in other states we qualify to Natural Rally we come here

If the today's Closing Price is greater than NaturalReaction price plus threshold then

Record the following new prices;

NaturalReactionRL[4] equals NaturalReaction; {Rule 4b}

If the today's Closing Price greater than UpTrend price then

{We resume the UpTrend}

{Rules 6d, 6f}

Mark the price down as always

UpTrend price equals today's Closing Price;

If we adhere to Rule10 then ResumeUpTrend equals true;

If today's Closing Price greater than NaturalRallyBL[5] plus HalfThreshold then

We begin {Rules 5a}

UpTrend price equals today's Closing Price;

If UseRule10 then mark ResumeUpTrend equals true;

If today's Closing Price less than DnTrend price then

{We change the state to Down Trend}

We begin {Rule 6b}

DownTrend price equals today's Closing Price

{This always happens with recording the last price}

NaturalRallyBL[6] equals today's closing price; {rule 4D}

If today's Closing Price greater than the NaturalRally minus Threshold then

If today's Closing Price less than NaturalReaction) then

{Start Natural Reaction}

---

[3] Mark new up-trend price with Red Line (RL) Pivot Point
[4] Natural reaction marked with Red Line (RL)
[5] Natural Rally marked with black in Black Line (BL)
[6] same as footnote 5

{We change the state to Natural Reaction}

We begin {rule 4d, 6b}

NaturalReaction equals today's Closing Price

NaturalRallyBL equals today's Closing Price; {rule 4D} {Pivot pt, Rule 9b}

Else {we start secondary reaction}

We begin {rule 6h}

{We change the state to Secondary Reaction}

Mark it: SecondaryReaction equals today's Closing Price;

If today's Closing Price greater than last Natural Rally price then mark a new price

NaturalRally equal today's Closing Price;

End {InNatRally}

When in Secondary Rally State

Whenever in other states we qualify to Secondary Rally State we come here

If the today's Closing Price greater than the last marked UpTrend price then

We begin {rules 6d, 6f}

{We change the state to Up Trend}

Mark the UpTrend price as today's Closing Price

If adhere to UseRule10 then ResumeUpTrend mark as true;

If today's Closing Price greater than last marked NaturalRallyBL plus halfthreshold

Then we can begin {rules 5a}

{We change the state to Up Trend}

Mark the UpTrend price as today's Closing Price

If UseRule10 then ResumeUpTrend marked as true;

If today's Closing Price greater than the last marked NaturalRally price then

We begin {rule 6g}

{We change the state to Natural Rally}

..And of course mark the Natural Rally price as today's Closing Price;

If today's Closing Price less than the last marked DnTrend price then

{Start of a downtrend}

We begin {rule 6b}

{We change the state to Down Trend}

Mark the DnTrend price, as today's Closing Price;

Mark it - NaturalRallyBL price as today's Closing Price;

{Rule 4d, pivot pt, rule 9b}

If the today's Closing Price is greater than the SecondaryRally price

Then {record the higher high}

Mark it - SecondaryRally equals today's Closing Price; {rule 3, 6g}

End {InSecRally}

When in Down Trend State

Whenever in other states we qualify to Down Trend we come here

If today's Closing Price less than the NaturalRally - Threshold then

Mark it - NaturalRallyBL equal NaturalRally; {rule 4d}

If we adhere to ResumeDnTrend rule then {Rule 10 logic}

Compare if today's Closing Price less than (DownTrendBL minus HalfThreshold

Then

Mark ResumeDnTrend Rule as false; {rule 10a}

Record DownTrend as equals today's Closing Price {rule 2, 6b}

If today's Closing Price less than DnTrendBL plus HalfThreshold then

{DnTrend Over}

{Return to NaturalRally}

{We change the state to Natural Rally}

Mark NaturalRally as today's Closing Price;

If today's Closing Price greater than DnTrend plus Threshold

Then {Start Natural Rally}

We begin {rules 4c, 6c}

{We change the state to Natural Rally}

Record NaturalRally as equals today's Closing Price;

DnTrendBL equals DownTrend; {Pivot Pt, Rule 8}

Mark ResumeDnTrend as false;

If today's Closing Price is less than the last DownTrend column

Then this means that we remain in down trend, record lower lows

Mark DonwTrend as equals today's Closing Price;

{Rule 2, 6b}

End; {InDnTrend}

When in Natural Reaction State

Whenever in other states we qualify to Natural Reaction we come here

Let's begin   {Natural Reaction State}

If today's Closing Price less than the NaturalRally minus Threshold then

Mark it - NaturalRallyBL as NaturalRally; {Rule 4d}

If today's Closing Price less than the DownTrend) then

We resume the DownTrend

Lets begin {Rule 6b, 6e}

{We change the state to DownTrend}

Mark DownTrend as today's Closing Price;

If UseRule10 then ResumeDnTrend set true;

If today's Closing Price less than the NaturalReactionRL minus halfthreshold

Then we can {Resume DownTrend}

Let's begin {rules 5b}

{We change the state to DownTrend}

Set DownTrend to today's Closing Price;

If UseRule10 then mark ResumeDnTrend as true;

If today's Closing Price greater than the UpTrend then {start UpTrend}

Let's begin {rule 6d}

{We change the state to UpTrend}

Set UpTrend to today's Closing Price;

Mark NaturalReactionRL as today's Closing Price

{Rule 4b, pivot point, rule 9c}

If today's Closing Price > NaturalReaction plus Thresh) then also check

If today's Closing Price > NaturalRally) then {start Natural Rally}

Lets begin {rules 4b, 6d}

{We change the state to Natural Rally}

Mark NaturalRally as today's Closing Price;

Also Mark NaturalReactionRL today's Closing Price;

{Rule 4b, pivot point, rule 9c}

Else {start SecondaryRally}

Let's begin {rule 6g}

{We change the state to Secondary Rally}

Mark SecondaryRally as today's Closing Price;

If today's Closing Price less than the NaturalReaction

Then we remain in NaturalReaction State, and record lower lows

Mark NaturalReaction as today's Closing Price {rule 3, 6a, 6b}

End; {InNatReact}

When in Secondary Reaction State

If today's Closing Price less than the DownTrend

Then {resume DownTrend}

Lets begin {rules 6b, 6e}

{We change the state to Down Trend}

Mark DownTrend to today's Closing Price

If UseRule10 then ResumeDnTrend set true;

If today's Closing Price less than the last NaturalReactionRL minus halfthreshold then

Let's begin {rules 5b}

{We change the state to Down Trend}

Mark the DownTrend to today's Closing Price;

If we adhere to Rule10 then mark ResumeDnTrend as true;

If today's Closing Price greater than the last recorded UpTrend

Then {start UpTrend}

Let's begin {rules 6d}

{We change the state to Up Trend}

Mark UpTrend as today's Closing Price;

Mark NaturalReactionRL to as today's Closing Price; {rule 4b, pivot point, rule 9c}

If today's Closing Price greater than the NaturalReaction

Then we begin {rules 6h}

{We change the state to Up Trend}

Mark NaturalReaction as today's Closing Price;

If today's Closing Price less than the SecondaryReaction then {record lower lows}

    Mark SecondaryReaction as today's Closing Price {rule 6h}

End; {InSecReact}

Buy Sell Rules

If we are in up-trend

    If we have no open position then

        Buy At Market next day at open

    If we have open short position then

        Cover At Market next day at open

If we are in a downtrend

    If we have no open position then

        Short At Market next day at the open

    If we have a long position open then

        Sell At Market next day at the open

Clearly it is not advisable to trade the reactions no matter how enticing they may be. My testing shows that occasional short-term trades may be profitable when trading reactions and short term rallies. It is best to trade only clear trends and exit when the trends change.

Important Concepts

Essentially the Market Key Livermore developed *is* the double top and inversely the double bottom market technicians later started learning about.

The market key system hinges on the threshold and the method of its calculation.

For stock we can use 6 points [7], for futures we should use ATR.

I have tested the points based system and obviously it was not working on futures.

There are two ways to trade – one is buy on pullbacks in existing trends, the other is a more profitable and risky, identify market turns as early as possible. This is what Livermore did. He added on pullbacks but seldom established the initial position there.

The essence of the Livermore market key is more than the pivotal points and reversal

It's all about the "soul" of the machine. With his system you will be able to tell if there is a CHANGE happening ... way before it becomes obvious. <u>And that is the edge you'll ever need.</u>

Concept 1

Focus on the market first and stock selection second.

While both efforts are important focusing on one stock for the bull move would be self-defeating on the extreme bearish day.

I suspect the reason that Mr. Livermore emphasizes this core truth of speculation so much is because it is so contrary to our natural inclinations as speculators. We tend to want to ignore the markets as a whole and focus on the exciting story stocks, always looking for the next future giant like Microsoft while it is still in its infant stage.

Yet, if we spend so much time focusing on individual stocks that our current understanding of the big strategic market picture fades, we risk losing the forest for the trees.

Concept 2
Do not rely on others for opinion.

Never trade on information from an anonymous or unaccountable source, such as some random e-mail touting a stock, or some unknown poster on the Web hiding behind a false name, or even a friend of a friend of a friend. Always be wary of someone who appears to be just picking stocks for the sake of picking stocks, with no strategic market context offered. And if someone presents a case for a stock that is just too good to be true, then it probably isn't true. Livermore was notorious in his intense dislike towards tipsters and other bottom feeder species. Of course nowadays with CNBC, technical analyst and other assorted gurus you can hardly avoid external ideas. You do not however have to act on them.

Concept 3

"Do not give it away"

This is perhaps the most important of all the Livermore rules. You can follow everything and be always right about the market and timing it. If you sell out your winning positions too soon you will not make it on the long run. Even if you scratch a living as a trader, making it big (i.e. rich) will be impossible.

Concept 4

Have a System

Livermore was perhaps the first system trader in the era when personal computers were non-existent. He must have had a phenomenal memory and keen sense of numbers. Once he saw his system provided a tremendous edge he would guard it as State secret.

Concept 5

The speculator's chief enemies are always boredom from within

Once he had money Livermore famously entertained his soul with fine living and the opposite sex. He knew that boredom leads to disaster, and gambling. Yachting and other entertainment is always better than over-trading.

---

[7] For stocks we need to adjust this depending of the price ($6 is for a $30 stock)

Concept 6

Use money management

This concept is where Livermore's weakness lied. He traded too big when he felt right and of course often he somehow managed to go broke. He believed the idea that never risk more than 10-percent of your bankroll

Concept 7

Establish entry and exit points and understand risk reward rations

This is almost as crucial as the *patience and waiting* part. If the trader can't grasp the risk reward for each and every trade he/she enters getting to the "big home runs" may never come.

Concept 8

Do not look at quotes during the day

Livermore did not always adhere to this concept but the message is clear - day trading was a bad idea back then as it is now. Intraday fluctuations may confuse and shake the trader no matter how resolved he/she may be. It is better to have a smaller position and let it work it's way than have a too large position that you are scared to leave and take home overnight.

Market Key Rules

Rule 1). When prices were in Upward Trend Livermore recorded them in black ink. In the paint-bar study we use blue annotation for up-trending prices.

Rule 2). When prices were in a Downward Trend Livermore recorded them in red ink. In the paint-bar study we use red annotation for down trending prices.

Rule 3). The other four prices were to be recorded are Natural Reaction Price, Secondary Reaction, Natural Rally, Secondary Rally.

Rule 4) (a). If the price was not upward trend (but it was) it must be assumed that it is a Natural Reaction State approximately 6 points away from the last recorded Upward Trend price.

Rule 4) (b). The Natural Reaction was to be recorded in red ink (in our case Purple) the first day you started recording prices in the Natural Rally or in the Up-trend column. You do this on the first rally of approximately 6 points recorded from the Natural Reaction column.

Now Livermore had two pivotal points to watch the last price of the up trend and the last price of the natural reaction. Watching these pivotal prices and the following price action ensuing allowed him to form an opinion if the trend is to continue or has ended.

Rule 4) (c). Livermore drew black lines under your last recorded price in the downtrend column the first day you started recording the Natural Rally. He begun to do this on the first rally of approximately six points from the last recorded downtrend price.

Rule 4) (d). He drew black lines under his last recorded price in the natural rally column on the first day he started to record figures in the natural reaction column or in the down trend column. He started this on the first reaction of approximately six points from the last price in the natural rally column.

Rule 5) (a). When the Natural Rally price is three or more points above the last Natural Rally pivotal price (the one marked with black ink), then this price should be entered in black ink into the Up Trend column.

Rule 5) (b). When recording the Natural Reaction column and the price has reached that is the three more points below the Natural Reaction column (marked with red ink – signifying a pivotal price) that price should be entered in the downtrend column.

Rule 6) (a). When a reaction occurs to an extent of approximately six points, after you have been recording prices in the Up-trend column, you then start to enter these prices in the Natural Reaction column. Continue to do so as long as the price recorder is lower than the last recorded Natural Reaction.

Rule 6) (b). When a reaction occurs to an extent of six points, after you have been recording prices in the Natural Rally column. You then start recording these prices in the Natural Reaction column. Continue doing so as log as the price is lower the last recorded Natural Reaction price.

Rule 6) (c). When a rally occurs to an extent of six points, after you have been recording prices in the Downtrend column. You then start record these prices in the Natural Rally column. Continue doing so as long as the price is higher than the last recorded price in the Natural Rally.

Rule 6) (d). When a rally occurs to an extent of six points, after you have been recording prices in the Natural reaction column. Now you start recording the prices in the Natural rally and do so as long as the price recorded is higher than the last recorded Natural Rally price. In case the price has made a higher high than last recorded in the Up-trend column – record this price as the new Up-trend price.

Rule 6) (e). When you start recording prices in the Natural Reaction column and the price is a lower low than the last recorded Down-trend price than this lower low becomes the new Down-trend price and you must record it so.

Rule 6) (f). Same rule applies when you record prices in the Natural Rally column. When the price is a higher high than the last recorded Up-trend price than you stop recording the natural rally column and record that price in black ink in the Up-trend column.

Rule 6) (f). When you have been recording in the Natural Reaction column and a rally should occur from the last recorded Natural Reaction (pivot price) to the extent of six points. If this price does not reach the last recorded Natural Rally price (other pivot) then this price must be recorded as a Secondary Rally. You should continue recording in the Secondary Rally column as long as the price recorded has not reached (and extended) to the last figure recorded in the Natural Rally column. When and if this occurs you should commence recording prices in the Natural Rally column again.

Rule 6) (h). In case you are recording in the Natural Rally column and a reaction should occur of approximately six points, but the price of the reaction was not lower than the last recorded price in the Natural Reaction price column. This price should be entered in the Secondary reaction column. You should continue recording the Secondary Reaction price as long as the price is lower than the last recorded Natural Reaction price. Once we reached and extended the last Natural Reaction we should then commence recording the price in the Natural Reaction and cease recording it as Secondary Reaction.

Rule 7). The same rules applies when recording the Key Price with the exception that the key price is twelve points

Rule 8). The last price recorded in the down or up trend becomes the pivotal point as soon as you start recording prices in Natural Rally or Natural Reaction columns.

Rule 9). Livermore saw the trend change in terms of color of his markings. When he saw black lines below prices below the last recorded red ink price he knew that the market might be turning.

Rule 10). This system is predicated on the premise that after the first Natural rally or Reaction has occurred the stock should resume the trend if there is to be a trend, that is. This rule is used in the software with a switch, to turn on and off this feature. If rule 10 was implemented in our testing the results was not that good. I am not sure if this is a result of some limitation of the software (state management glitch) or inherent problem understanding this part if the system.

The Life of Jesse Livermore

Jesse Livermore, though he died over sixty years ago, is still known today as one of the most colorful, flamboyant and respected market speculators of all time.

Known by such nicknames such as *Boy Plunger*, the *Great Bear* or *The Wall Street Wonder* and the *Cotton King*. Livermore both made, and subsequently lost, four multi-million dollar fortunes during his career as a speculator, which lasted over three decades.

Livermore was an early starter. He went to work at age 16 as a stock quotation boy for a local firm. He must have found his calling early as numbers came very easy for him and he must have had a great, almost perfect memory recall to remember earlier days activities.

He finished 4 years of math in one while working as a quote boy at the local Broker's office.

It is a fact that Livermore went broke three times before reaching the age 30. The amazing thing is that he had the mental strength and toughness to come back.

His psychology is one of the most fascinating case studies of all great speculators. He suffered from severe mood swings and trading actually gave him a solace and meaning.

Ari Kiev, a well-known psychologist for traders has a following in his book that can be applied to Jesse Livermore very accurately.

""According to Joseph Campbell, the late authority on mythology, the more challenging a situation is, the greater the stature of the person whom can assimilate it. 'The demon that you can swallow gives you its power, and the greater life's pain, the greater life's reply.' This applies to trading--the more discomfort you experience, the more effective you will be as a trader."

Interesting thing about Livermore, if he was depressed he remained fairly "balanced" in his trading activities even when hitting the highs or the lows of spectacular gain and losses.

So my conclusion is that I don't think it was trading that did him in, but life, aging and probably women.

Of course his last loss the biggest that made him an average person of no great wealth from 100 million of 1929 dollars that is the equivalent of billions of today's currency could be unsettling at least to say.

Livermore set-up trusts for his wife and children in the early 20's. Trusts that were so tight, that neither he, nor his wife/children, would ever be able to penetrate them.

Observers' one criticism of Livermore was that Livermore had only studied how to make money - not how to keep money. In other words "He had the greed and the drive for power, and when he got a large amount of money, he could not trade conservatively. He tried to make the market go his way instead of waiting until the market was ready to follow the natural trend".

Livermore's success gave him a lifestyle that many could only dream about. The tall, thin blonde speculator bought a 200-foot yacht, the Anita. He dated famous women, including actress Lillian Russell. His trading exploits soon became well known, and people would often comment that someone was "as rich as Jesse Livermore".

Brief Chronology of Livermore's life;

By 1900, aged 23, he had amassed roughly $50,000, from the bucket shops.

Fall of 1905 Thomas Lawson of Boston provided all partnership capital for Livermore to raid Union Pacific stock. Actively traded by Harriman. pool.

Losing his ass up until April 18, 1906 San Francisco earthquake. Stock took two days to respond lower. Lawson got the proceeds and Livermore pocketed $300,000 Took off for Saratoga.

On an unknown date soon after Livermore made the mistake of going short the SAME stock. Harriman pool was prepared. Livermore watched a quarter of a million vanish on upticks.

Another 50/50 deal with Lawson to short Great Northern. Made a second killing. .

Made his FIRST million in shorting Anaconda in the summer of 1907. This win was due to Market panic as much as his skill. The Banks were calling existing loans. October 24, 1907 J.P. Morgan forced his fellow capitalists to start supporting stocks. Livermore knew better than to buck the Morgan crowd. Bought his first yacht, the Anita Venetian.

Had an epiphany that commodities posed less "problems" because prices depended upon supply and demand (rather than synthetic measures). He was a Long 120,000 bale of cotton. First used the power of the press release. In the New York Herald "July Cotton Cornered by Jesse Livermore". Shorts covered, suckers (his term) rushed in, Livermore unloaded. Hence the new nickname, Cotton King.

Spring of 1908, Desperately trying to stem a dropping price by buying in both New Orleans and Liverpool, found himself long 500,000 bales. Simply put, the Anita Venetian went under the hammer.

For Livermore 1911-1913 appear to be lean years.

In 1914 he was living Bretton Hall Hotel at 86th & Broadway.

Filed bankruptcy in 1915 with $102,474 in professed liabilities.

The Bethlehem Steel trade in LeFevere's book was in here somewhere.

December 20, 1916, somehow became alerted to a telegram to Finlay Barrel & Co. in Palm Beach from a Washington reporter named W.W. Price leaking of Wilson warning the warring parties. Figuring there'd be a market collapse, Livermore approached Lawson again. With capital, shorted the "four horsemen" US Steel, American Can, Baldwin, and Anaconda. E.F Hutton made a flash wire to its offices hours before Wilson's note was publicized. Bids melted away. Livermore bought a half million annuity to throw off $30,000 per annum Also rushed out and bought a speed boat called the 'sub-catcher" and a $120,000 platinum and emerald ring.

Unloaded his first wife via Reno in October 1917 and the 40 year on December 2, 1918 old married the 18 year old daughter of a wealthy Brooklyn merchant named Wendt. Rented a furnished townhouse at 8 West 76th Street. January 1920, bought a seat on the Curb (today the AMEX). 1919, first son arrives.

1921 had a pool agreement with the Lewisohn Brothers to ramp Seneca Copper. After running from $12 to $25, the brothers cancelled the (then legal) agreement.

Summer of 1922, Livermore was reported to have lost $8.5 million on the short side of Mexican Pete. June 1922, Clarence Saunders, owner of the Piggly Wiggly chain hired Livermore to "kill the bears". By November, Livermore had amassed 105,000 of 200,000 shares outstanding at an average of $35. March 1923, stock was over $70. Livermore had 198,872 of the float. March 19th, Saunders asked Livermore to spring the trap demanding delivery from short sellers. Livermore reneged. Suander's somehow succeeded anyway. From an open of 75 ½ skyrockets to $124, and closed the day at $82. Same year ran the Mammoth Oil pool involving Harry Sinclair.

In 1924, Arthur Cutten forced wheat to over $2 per bushel for the first time. Livermore was short and lost a considerable amount.

In 1927, Livermore ran a pool to ramp Freeport Texas stock from $19 to $74 ½. Also a director of Minter & Assoc, selling $9 million worth of Florida lots and filing BK two years after inception. Robbed at gunpoint in his home in May 1927.

April 1929, sued for $1,450,000 over the 1926 Boca Raton RE crash.

July 1929 refused to make a court appearance in a $525,000 suit against him by the Carbonite Corp for an alleged breach of agreement.

October 1929, details sketchy but even though Livermore "won" millions on the short side, he lost $6 million in his long positions in the crash.. Arthur Cutten purportedly lost $50 million.

August 16, 1932. He divorced his second wife. March 28, 1933, married his third wife at age 56. May 30, 1933. Security Legislation enacted. Pool operations outlawed.

March 4, 1934, Livermore filed BK. $2,259,212 liabilities/$184,000 assets.

Thanksgiving Eve 1935 his divorced second wife shot his first son. Non-fatal.

Summer 1937 chartered a yacht (Nina) rather than owning it outright.

Apparently from 1934 to 1940 he was an investment advisor/broker. Apparently to acquire capital for a comeback, he decided to write a book (in two versions) the office that's frequently mentioned in awe appears to have been a facade to promote the book. The "legendary" market key is patterned after Dow Theory confirmation, but using two companies in each of about 5 leading industries. Not original, basically the opposite of pairs trading.

November 28, 1940, shot himself in the head in the hatcheck room of the Sherry-Netherland hotel after writing an 8-page note to his wife with the recurrent theme "My life has been a failure"

How to use the Code

Importing EasyLanguage Archive and Storage files (ELA and ELS Files)

{** ©1987, 1999 Omega Research, Inc. **}

(Using TradeStation 2000i)

When importing analysis techniques, you can only import one ELA/ELS file at a time. Each ELA/ELS file may contain several analysis techniques. Once you specify the file to import, the wizard enables you to select individually each analysis technique you want import from the file. If the analysis technique already exists in your product, the analysis technique is not imported.

To import an EasyLanguage Archive/Storage file:

1   Use the File - Import and Export menu sequence to open the Import and Export Wizard.

2   Click Import EasyLanguage Archive File (ELA and ELS).

3   Click Next.

4   In the Select the location of your EasyLanguage Archive file box, enter the appropriate path and file name (e.g., C:\My Analysis Techniques\Indicators.els).

Note If you do not know the location and/or path of your EasyLanguage Archive file, you can scan or browse your hard drive. For more information, see Scanning Your Hard Drive for EasyLanguage Archive Files.

5   Click Next.

6   Select the categories of analysis techniques you want to import.

Note Click Select All to select all analysis categories. Click Clear All to clear all categories so that you can reselect the appropriate categories.

7   Click Next.

8   Select the analysis technique(s) you want to import.

Note Click Select All to select all analysis techniques. Click Clear All to clear all analysis techniques so that you can reselect the appropriate analysis techniques.

9   Click Finish.

10   When the importing process is complete, click OK.

{** ©1987, 1999 Omega Research, Inc. **}

INSTRUCTIONS FOR "TRANSFER IN" TO TRADESTATION
(From TradeStation 4.0 Help File)

When you receive a disk or CD that contains an indicator, a ShowMe or PaintBar study, a trading system, or a function in ELA file format, do not use the Windows Explorer, the Windows File Manager, or the DOS COPY command to copy these analysis techniques into TradeStation. Instead, you must use TradeStation's transfer feature.
To transfer an analysis technique into TradeStation from another directory, a disk, or a CD, when it is in the ELA file format, use the following steps:

1. Use the Tools - QuickEditor menu sequence to access the QuickEditor.

2. Click the Transfer button to produce the Transfer Analysis Techniques dialog.

3. Click the Transfer analysis techniques FROM Easy Language Archive file radio button to transfer in analysis techniques.

4. Click on OK to produce the Transfer from archive file dialog.

5. In the From edit box, enter the complete path name for and the name of the Easy Language Archive file (.ELA) from which you want to transfer the analysis techniques. Enter the path name and file name using one of the following methods:

a) If you have previously transferred files, TradeStation remembers where the ELA files were located and lists the ELA file names in the From drop-down list. Choose an ELA file from the drop-down list.

b) In the From edit box, type in the drive letter, the correct path name, and the ELA file name. For example, C:\TEMP\SYSTEMS, where C: is the drive letter, TEMP is the directory path name, and SYSTEMS is the ELA file name TradeStation is to create.

c) Click on the Browse button to access the standard Windows Open dialog, in which you can choose the directory and the ELA file that contains the analysis techniques you want to transfer in. Once you specify the file and click OK, the information is placed in the From edit box.

d) Click the Scan button to have TradeStation scan any drive you specify for existing ELA files. Any ELA files found are placed in the From drop-down list. You can then choose the ELA file that contains the analysis techniques you want to transfer in from the drop-down list.

6. Once you enter the information in the From edit box, click on OK to produce the Transfer dialog.

7. Click on the radio button for the type of analysis technique you want to transfer into TradeStation. You may transfer in only one type of analysis technique at a time, unless you select Transfer All and transfer in all the analysis techniques found in the ELA file. If the radio button for a particular type of analysis technique is dimmed (grayed-out), it means TradeStation did not find that type of analysis technique in the ELA file you specified.

8. Once you select either the specific analysis technique type or Transfer All, click on OK. Unless you have a specific reason for doing otherwise we seriously recommend that you use the Transfer All option in order to be sure that all the included user functions are transferred with the system code.

a) If you selected Transfer All, TradeStation begins transferring in the analysis techniques contained in the ELA file you specified. If an analysis technique with the same name as one you are transferring in already exists in TradeStation, a warning dialog will appear indicating that the duplicate analysis technique was not transferred.
OR
b) If you selected a specific type of analysis technique, the Transfer analysis technique type dialog appears.

Click on as many analysis techniques as you want to transfer in; this highlights the technique. To deselect an analysis technique, click on it again.
Once you have highlighted the analysis techniques you want to transfer in, click on OK. TradeStation begins transferring the analysis techniques from the ELA file into TradeStation. If an analysis technique with the same name as one you are transferring in already exists in TradeStation, a warning dialog will appear indicating that the duplicate analysis technique was not transferred.

9. When TradeStation is finished transferring the analysis techniques in from the ELA file, you are returned to the QuickEditor. Click Close to return to TradeStation.

You can now insert the analysis technique into your TradeStation chart. For information on inserting the different analysis techniques into your chart window, refer to the sections that cover indicators, ShowMe and PaintBar studies, and trading systems. How to work with user functions is covered in the Easy Language User's Manual.

INSTRUCTIONS FOR LOADING SYSTEMS INTO SUPERCHARTS 4.0

(Older versions do not use the Ela format and cannot use this technique. See below for versions prior to 4.0
(From SuperCharts 4.0 Help File)

When you receive a disk or CD that contains an indicator, a ShowMe or PaintBar study, a trading system, or a function in ELA file format, do not use the Windows Explorer, the Windows File Manager, or the DOS COPY command to copy these analysis techniques into SuperCharts. Instead you must use SuperCharts transfer feature.

To transfer an analysis technique into SuperCharts from another directory, a disk, or a CD, when it is in the ELA file format, use the following steps:

1. Use the Tools - QuickEditor menu sequence to access the QuickEditor.

2. Click the Transfer button to produce the Transfer Analysis Techniques dialog.

3. Click the Transfer analysis techniques FROM Easy Language Archive file radio button to transfer in analysis techniques.

4. Click on OK to produce the Transfer from archive file dialog.

5. In the 'From' edit box, enter the complete path name for and the name of the Easy Language Archive file (.ELA) from which you want to transfer the analysis techniques. Enter the path name and file name using one of the following methods:

a) If you have previously transferred files, SuperCharts remembers where the ELA files were located and lists the ELA file names in the 'from' drop-down list. Choose an ELA file from the drop-down list.

b) In the 'From' edit box, type in the drive letter, the correct path name, and the ELA file name. For example, C:\TEMP\SYSTEMS, where C: is the drive letter, TEMP is the directory path name, and SYSTEMS is the ELA file name SuperCharts is to create.

c) Click on the Browse button to access the standard Windows Open dialog, in which you can choose the directory and the ELA file that contains the analysis techniques you want to transfer in. Once you specify the file and click OK, the information is placed in the 'From' edit box.

d) Click the Scan button to have SuperCharts scan any drive you specify for existing ELA files. Any ELA files found are placed in the From drop-down list. You can then choose the ELA file that contains the analysis techniques you want to transfer in from the drop-down list.

6. Once you enter the information in the 'From' edit box, click on OK to produce the Transfer dialog.

7. Click on the radio button for the type of analysis technique you want to transfer into SuperCharts. You may transfer in only one type of analysis technique at a time, unless you select Transfer All and transfer in all the analysis techniques found in the ELA file. If the radio button for a particular type of analysis technique is dimmed (grayed-out), it means SuperCharts did not find that type of analysis technique in the ELA file you specified.

8. Once you select either the specific analysis technique type or Transfer All, click on OK.

a) If you selected Transfer All, SuperCharts begins transferring in the analysis techniques contained in the ELA file you specified. If an analysis technique with the same name as one you are transferring in already exists in SuperCharts, a warning dialog will appear indicating that the duplicate analysis technique was not transferred.

OR

b) If you selected a specific type of analysis technique, the Transfer analysis technique type dialog appears.

Click on as many analysis techniques as you want to transfer in; this highlights the technique. To deselect an analysis technique, click on it again. Once you have highlighted the analysis techniques you want to transfer in, click on OK. SuperCharts begins transferring the analysis techniques from the ELA file into SuperCharts. If an analysis technique with the same name as one you are transferring in already exists in SuperCharts, a warning dialog will appear indicating that the duplicate analysis technique was not transferred.

9. When SuperCharts is finished transferring the analysis techniques in from the ELA file, you are returned to the QuickEditor. Click Close to return to SuperCharts.

You can now insert the analysis technique into your SuperCharts chart. For information on inserting the different analysis techniques into your chart window, refer to the sections that cover indicators, ShowMe and PaintBar studies, and trading systems. How to work with functions is covered in the Easy Language User's Manual.

INSTRUCTIONS FOR IMPORTING ANALYSIS TECHNIQUES IN TRADESTATION 2000I

We have supplied the code for the system in both ela, Tradestation 4.0 format and els TradeStation 200i format. Use the els file if you are importing into Tradestation 2000i, and be sure to select all, when prompted.

When importing analysis techniques, you can only import one ELA/ELS file at a time. Each ELA/ELS file may contain several analysis techniques. Once you specify the file to import, the wizard enables you to select individually each analysis technique you want import from the file. If the analysis technique already exists in your product, the analysis technique is not imported.

To import an EasyLanguage Archive/Storage file:

1   Use the File - Import and Export menu sequence to open the Import and Export Wizard.

2   Click Import EasyLanguage Archive File (ELA and ELS).

3   Click Next.

4   In the Select the location of your EasyLanguage Archive File box, enter the appropriate path and file name (e.g., C:\My Analysis Techniques\Indicators.els).

Note If you do not know the location and/or path of your EasyLanguage Archive file, you can scan or browse your hard drive. For more information, see Scanning Your Hard Drive for EasyLanguage Archive Files.

5   Click Next.

6   Select the categories of analysis techniques you want to import.

Note: Click Select All to select all analysis categories. Click Clear All to clear all categories so that you can reselect the appropriate categories.

7   Click Next.

8   Select the analysis technique(s) you want to import.

Note: Click Select All to select all analysis techniques. Click Clear All to clear all analysis techniques so that you can reselect the appropriate analysis techniques.

9   Click Finish.

10   When the importing process is complete, click OK.

INSTRUCTIONS FOR INSERTING ANALYSIS TECHNIQUES

Analysis techniques, which include Indicators, ShowMe studies, PaintBar studies and trading systems, can be inserted only on an active chart window. To make a chart window active, simply click on it or use the Window menu.

Once your chart window is active, you can add an analysis technique to it in any of three ways: the Menu Sequence method, the Shortcut menu method, or the Indicator icon method. The following covers each of these three methods.

Using the Menu Sequence Method

Use the following directions to insert analysis techniques in your chart window using the menu sequence method:

1. Use the Insert - Analysis Techniques menu sequence to produce the Insert Analysis Techniques dialog, shown below. This dialog contains four tabs.

Insert Analysis Techniques dialog

2. Click on the appropriate tab to produce the corresponding dialog. For example, to insert an indicator, click the Indicator tab.

3. Select one analysis technique by clicking on it, or more than one analysis technique by holding down the CTRL key and clicking on the analysis techniques you wish to apply.

If you want to format the analysis technique (change inputs, color, style, scaling, and other properties) before it is plotted, click in the Format checkbox to place a check mark in the box. (To remove the check mark click again.)

4. Click the Plot button. You are returned to the chart window. The analysis has been applied to the chart.

If you chose to format your analysis technique before inserting it on the chart window, the Format analysis technique dialog is produced when you click the Plot button. After specifying the way you want the analysis technique to be displayed, click the OK button to insert the analysis technique and return to the chart window.

Using the Shortcut Menu Method

The following covers using the Shortcut menu method to insert an analysis technique in your chart.

1. Place the mouse pointer on any empty area of the chart window and click the right mouse button to produce the Shortcut menu shown below.

Chart window Shortcut menu

2. Select Insert Analysis Techniques to produce the Insert Analysis Techniques dialog.
2. Click on the appropriate tab to produce the corresponding dialog. For example, to insert an indicator, click the Indicator tab.
3. Select one analysis technique by clicking on it, or more than one analysis technique by holding down the CTRL key and clicking on the analysis techniques you wish to apply.

If you want to format the analysis technique (change inputs, color, style, scaling, and other properties) before it is plotted, click in the Format checkbox to place a check mark in the box. (To remove the check mark click again.)

4. Click the Plot button. You are returned to the chart window. The analysis has been applied to the chart.

If you chose to format your analysis technique before inserting it on the chart window, the Format analysis technique dialog is produced when you click the Plot button. After specifying the way you want the analysis technique to be displayed, click the OK button to insert the analysis technique and return to the chart window.

The Wealth-lab code you can just cut and paste into the Wealth-lab developer 3.0 edit widow after you press on the new strategy icon. If in doubt please consult your WLD manual or guide.

Quotes to Remember

These are the best of *Reminiscence of a Stock Operator.*

On Page 10

"Another lesson I learned early is that there is nothing new in Wall Street. There can't be because speculation is as old as the hills. Whatever happens in the stock market today has happen before and will happen again."

On Page 11

"The reason for what a certain stock does today may not be known for two or there days, or weeks, or months… But you must act instantly or be left."

On Page 21

"What beat me was not having brains enough to stick to own game—that is , to play the market only when I was satisfied that precedents favored my play. There is a time for all things, but I didn't know it."

"There is the plain fool who does the wrong thing at all times everywhere, but there is the Wall Street fool, who thinks he must trade all the time."

On Page 22

"The Desire for constant action irrespective of underlying conditions is responsible for many losses in Wall Street even among the professionals, who feel that they must take home some money everyday, as though they were working for regular wages."

On Page 36

"But there is only one side to the stock market; and it is not the bull side or the bear side, but the right side."

"A man must believe in himself and his judgment if he expects to make a living at this game."

On Page 39

"We not only ran into an era of industrial consolidations and combinations of capital that had beaten anything we had up to that time, but the public went stock mad."

On Page 59

"I was twenty when I made my first ten thousand and I lost that. But I knew how and why-because I traded out of season all the time; because when I couldn't play according to my system, which was based on study and experience, I went and gambled. I hoped to win instead of knowing that I ought to win on form."

"There is nothing like losing all you have in the world for teaching you what not to do. And when you know what not to do in order not to lose money, you begin to learn what not to do in order to win. Did you get that? You begin to learn."

On Page 60

"If a stock doesn't act right don't touch it; because being unable to tell precisely what is wrong, you cannot tell which way it is going. No diagnosis, no prognosis. No prognosis, no profit."

On Page 61

"I should say that a chart helps those you can read it or rather who can assimilate what they read. The average chart reader, however, is apt to become obsessed with the notion that the dips and peaks and primary and secondary movements are all there is to stock speculation. If he pushes his confidence to its logical limit he is bound to go broke."

On Page 62

"I didn't expect to do as well as I did in the bucket shops, but I though after a while I would do much better because I would be able to swing a much heavier line. Yet I can see now that my main trouble was failure to grasp the vital difference between stock gambling and stock speculating."

On Page 63

"It was the change in my own attitude that was of supreme importance to me. It taught me, little by little, the essential difference between betting on fluctuations and anticipating inevitable advances and declines, between gambling and speculating."

On Page 68

"I think it was a long step forward in my trading education when I realized at last that that when old Mr. Partridge kept on telling the other the other customers. "Well, you know this is a bull market!" he really meant to tell them that the big money was not in the individual fluctuations but in the main movements – that is, not in reading the tape but in sizing up the entire market and its trend."

"It never was my thinking that made the big money for me. It always was sitting. Got that? My sitting tight!"

"… It is no trick at all to be right on the market… I've known many men who were right at exactly the right time and began buying or selling stocks at exactly the right time…"

And there experience invariably matched mine—that is, they made no real money out of it.

On Page 69

"Men who can both be right and sit tight are uncommon. I found it one of the hardest things to learn. But it is only after a stock operator has firmly grasped this that he can make big money. It is literally true that millions come easier to a trader after he knows how to trade than hundreds did in the days of his ignorance."

"In a bull market your game is to buy and hold until you believe that the bull market is near its end. To do this must study general conditions and not tips or special factors affecting individual stocks. Then get out of all your stocks; get out for keeps!"

On Page 77

"The tape doesn't lie, does it?" "It doesn't always tell the truth on the instant," I said

On Page 83

"It was not that all I needed to learn was not to take tips but follow my own inclination. It was that I gained confidence in myself and I was able finally to shake off the old method of trading."

On Page 84

"But the average man doesn't wish to be told that it is a bull or a bear market. What he desires is to be told specifically which particular stock to buy or sell. He wants to get something for nothing. He does not wish to work. He doesn't even wish to think."

"Well I wasn't that lazy but I found it easier to think of individual stocks than of the general market and therefore of individual fluctuations rather that than of general movements. I had to change that and I did."

On Page 109

"The big men of the Street are prone to wishful thinkers as the politicians or the plain suckers. In a speculator such an attitude is fatal."

On Page 111

"For a sucker play a man gets sucker pay."

On Page 123

"At 164 prices looked mighty high, but as I told you before, stocks are never too high to buy or too low to sell."

On Page 126

"Do you wish to gamble blindly in the hope of getting a great big profit or do you wish to speculate intelligently and get a smaller but much more probable profit?"

On Page 130

"The successful trader has to fight these two deep-seated instincts. He has to reverse what you might call his natural impulses. Instead of hoping he must fear; instead of fearing he must hope. He must fear his loss may develop into a much bigger loss, and hope that his profit may become a much bigger profit."

On Page 180

"Nowhere does history indulge it repetitions so often or so uniformly as is Wall Street."

"And there is anther thing to remember, and that is that a market does not culminate in one grand blaze of glory. Neither does it end with a sudden reversal of form."

On Page 183

"Never try to sell at the top. It isn't wise. Sell after a reaction if there is no rally."

On Page 184

"As I said before, in a bear market it is always wise to cover if complete demoralization suddenly develops."

On Page 247

"The first step in a bull movement in a stock is to advertise the fact that there is a bull movement on."

Money Management

Making it is often easier than keeping it.

Money and risk management, plus diversification, is interwoven with trend trading. There are rather long periods in which no ascertainable trends can be seen in a given market. This period eventually passes and some trend manages to re-establish itself. Trend trading mandates that we wait for these periods to pass and not trade until a strong trend is observed.

Pyramiding is relied upon. This amounts to using unrealized profits from a current market position to purchase additional contracts.

Unfortunately Jesse Livermore's strength was not his money management. He also live a lavish lifestyle that bordered manic grandiose of spending. For example for the 8th birthday of his son he hired the whole Circus for the weekend. I am sure that his psychological makeup had a great deal to do with this lifestyle.

Proof to Livermore's Achilles heel is Smitten's chapter 12 of Livermore's Money Management Rules (page 225 of Jesse Livermore: World Greatest Stock Trader", Wiley). This is about the most hollow and weakest chapter in the book. It describes a 10-precent cutoff for losses and taking profits off the table. These ideas are all fine but I suspect Livermore did not always follow them. On the positive side it is known that he established a trust for his family after his earlier run in with a 'bad patch' and losing it all.

You can also notice that Dennis' Risk Management system keeps your original stake (minus the 1-3 percent risk) and usually loses from money already made in the market. Hedge funds do not differentiate when taking losses into an account. Their system is marked to market and paper profits are considered real even if not yet taken.

Dennis was trading managed funds up until the middle of 2000. He had a big draw downs, about 40%, and closed up shop because the high water mark was quite big. He would need to make more than 65% before receiving a cent in performance fees. Assets at the time of closure were about $80 million, approx. half of that was his IIRC.

It is hard to prove this after so many years but my research indicates that Livermore's losses were a combination of breaking some of his own rules and an overspending lifestyle.

Stark contrast to Livermore was a later and almost engulfing success of Richard Dennis. Contrary to Livermore, Richard Dennis used stacks of Wall Street Journals as a chair and was known as a peculiar character, penchant for thrift in personal habits as in trading. When he (Dennis) lost big he lost mostly investor's money and managed to keep his stake intact.

The following money management system is taken from Richard Dennis and altered to use Livermore far more accurate signals for timing. Dennis used a 20-day and 55-day breakout that worked in commodities in the hyper inflationary times of the late seventies and eighties. UTS' (*Unit Trend System*) recommendation is to risk only up to 1-3% of funds on any given position.

To use Livermore's analogy for fishing - this technique may take small bites day in and day out while you constantly bait the line albeit with Livermore's entry/exit the drawdowns are less and more time is spent with observations and waiting for a turn. Using the indices and stock market the trends do not need to be as big and can be intermediate in nature.

For a large percentage of UTS trades, a finite loss of 1-3% will occur, just like in Turtle trading. They expect it, and UTS does as well. The winning trades, however, are expected to have a large "geometric" gain, due to pyramiding (as explained above) and catching a long trending move. The winning positions are expected to more than offset the many smaller losses.

General UTS Trading Rules

- Do not risk more than 1-3% of equity on any trade.
- Base position size on a formula (explained later, in discussion of ATR).
- Abandon any notion of profit goals in entering positions (Turtle concept).
- Be aggressive with profits. Do not use trailing stops. For example, if you have a 60% gain in soybeans, the stop loss is still set to the original 1-3%, meaning it is entirely possible the market will retrace all the way back to its original level and the paper profit would be lost (Turtle).
- As you start profiting in a position, begin increasing position size; when losses mount, decrease it (Turtle).

You have to be very daring with paper profits; most big money is made by huge market moves. Do you remember gold, when the high inflation of the 80's caused it to balloon to nearly $1000? Some traders profited in gold from the move $200 to $250, but missed the big move from $250 to $850! We don't want to miss out!

So, if true trailing stops are not followed, what will keep you from giving it all back (recall when silver crashed from $50/ounce to around $11)? UTS uses money management stops and time stops to exit positions (the latter is when a certain # of days passes during when a trade goes against you – more about this later).

Average True Range (ATR) Defined – An Essential Concept

Also referred to as the Trading Range, this system was introduced by J. Welles Wilder Jr. in his book "New Concepts in Technical Trading Systems." Wilder found that high ATR values often occur at market bottoms following a panic sell-off. Low ATR values are often found during extended sideways periods, such as those found at tops and after consolidations.

```
MA(TR, Type, Period)
TR = MAX{
   ABS(HI - LO),
   ABS(HI - CL.1),
   ABS(CL.1 - LO)
}
```

The True Range (TR) indicator is the greatest of the price difference from:

- today's high to today's low

- yesterday's close to today's high

- yesterday's close to today's low

The ATR is a moving average, typically 7 days, of the TRs. Refer to the attached atr.xls Excel worksheet for examples, to become more familiarized with this concept. Also, this concept can be applied using the spreadsheet formulas to historical data that has been supplied with the course. Import the data into spreadsheet format, and generate your own TR data, to reinforce the concepts presented here.

Why is TR so vital? It is a very important measuring block to make decisions on:

1☐ Number of contracts that make up each unit

2☐ Using stops

3☐ Determining when to pyramid (add additional units)

4☐ ATR peaks before price bottoms.

5☐ Low ATR means the market is ranging.

6☐ ATR peaks before the market top.

7☐ ATR peaks after a secondary rally.

8☐ ATR peaks during the early stages of a major price fall.

ATR Illustration

ATR is a truly adaptive and universal measure of market price movement. Here is an example that might help illustrate its flexibility. If we were to measure Corn's average price movement (i.e., volatility) over a two-day period and express this in dollars, it might be $500. If we were to measure the average price movement of a Yen contract, it would probably be about $2,000. If we were inventing a generalized technique to help us identify appropriate stop losses in Corn and Yen, it would have to generate two very different stop levels, because of the difference in volatility just demonstrated.

We might want a technique that would identify a $750 stop loss in Corn and a $3,000 stop loss in Yen, for example.

Assume that, using the information in the example, the ATR of Corn over a two-day period is $500 and the ATR of Yen over the same period is $2,000. If we were to use a stop expressed as 1.5 ATR, we could use the same formula for both markets! The Corn stop would be $750 and the Yen stop would be $3,000. Indeed, that is what we were looking for.

Now assume market conditions change, so Corn becomes extremely volatile and moves $1,000 over a two-day period and Yen gets very quiet and now moves only $1,000 over this two-day period. If still using our stops as originally expressed (not using our technique), we would still have a $750 stop in Corn (much too close now) and a $3,000 stop in Yen (much too far away now). However, our stop expressed in units of ATR would adapt to the changes, and our new "ATR stops" of 1.5 ATR would translate to $1,500 for both Corn and for Yen. We can now react to the new volatility and use these stops!

The ATR stops automatically adjust to market changes. Our new stop is 1.5 ATR; the formula is always the same. The value of using ATR as a universal and adaptive measure of market volatility cannot be overemphasized. ATR is an invaluable tool in building trading systems that are robust (meaning they are likely to work the same way in the future) and can be applied to many markets without modification. Using ATR, you might be able to build a system for Corn that actually works also in Yen, with the same formula. But perhaps more important, you can build a system using ATR that works well over your historical data, regardless of dramatic price fluctuations.

Risk Determination and using the Concept of Units

On average, trend following CTAs and big time traders use a risk figure that ranges from 1 % (conservative) to 3 % (aggressive).

Introduction to units and volatility

In futures, ATR can be measured in cents per bushel, dollars, pennies, whatever. Certain futures contracts have an ATR of 29 ticks, or $290, since each tick might equal $10.

To determine market volatility, you have to know the dollar amount per tick. Tick-size information is available on web-sites of the pertinent futures exchanges. They are not hard to find. In the example, the average daily range - the 1 ATR, is valued at $290. If a speculator has a $100,000 account with risk parameter of 1%, the unit size is $1000, with 10 units in the account. Divide this by one ATR, say $290, to get $1000 / $290 = 3.44 contracts. The purpose of this exercise is to show how we never go over our risk parameters.

By the way, if you have discipline, some decent trends and some money, it is very possible to become a millionaire using this trend-trading technique – just ask one of the Turtles. This is the only way to trade futures.

We are not through yet by a long shot, but a very short summary is in order: ATR acts as a measurement of funds at hand for a given risk tolerance. That's it, for now, but extremely important.

The problem with futures markets, as you may know already, is that tick sizes differ from contract to contract, as well as volatility.

To really comprehend the units' concept, when we take risk capital available and compute units per account, we force ourselves to adjust unit size depending on how much we have left. We must think in terms of units, not how much we have in dollars. The mistake of thinking in dollars is that we speculate with a horrendous leverage.

Trend Traders have a maximum unit rule: 10 total units, 5 units per market, 5-7 units per market group (i.e., soybean complex, bean, oil, meal), depending on a market group's correlation with another (more about this below, just before the Conclusion).

Unit Reduction Rule

Whenever you lose 10 ATR ($2,900 in our example) or 10% ($10,000 of the original $100,000), you must cut back the unit trading size by 20% (the new size would be $800, or 20% less than $1,000). This is pretty straightforward and objective.

Additional UTS Money Management Rules

- ☐ The system warrants that you never increase the quantity-traded in proportion to your equity growth.
- ☐ You need about 1/2 ATR average profit on all previous units before adding an additional unit to the total held in positions.
- ☐ It is strongly recommended to have all units on a position before it reaches

the 4 ATR mark. This should become obvious; pyramiding is dangerous when a move approaches an exhaustion point. Many traders lose money due to incorrect pyramiding.

☐ Trends tend to exhaust after reaching 10 ATR.

☐ Trade when volatility shrinks, to purchase more contracts for the same dollar risk.

☐ Exit profitable positions at different points (scale out).

How to Pyramid and Move-up Stops Properly using ATR

There are two ways of pyramiding. The safer way is when your initial position is larger than the subsequent position size added. As the price level gradually moves our way, the size added decreases. Hence the name pyramid. Trend traders should pyramid early on, since late pyramiding can be devastating on reversals. In this method, the average price is kept lower and unit risk is low.

Unit #	Unit Risk Exposure in ATR accumulation	Price	Final Stop level	New profit needed to pyram
1	2 ATR	X(initial price)	X	1/2 ATR
2	2 ATR + 1 1/2 ATR	X+1/2 ATR	X+1/2 ATR	1 ATR
3	2 ATR + 1 1/2 ATR + 1	X+1 ATR	X+1 ATR	1 1/2 ATR
4	2 ATR + 1 1/2 ATR + 1 + 1/2	X+1 1/2 ATR	X+1 1/2 ATR	2 ATR
5	2 ATR + 1 1/2 ATR + 1 + 1/2	X+2 ATR	X+2 ATR	2 1/2 ATR
6	2 ATR + 1 1/2 ATR + 1 + 1/2	X+2 1/2 ATR	X+2 1/2 ATR	3 ATR
7	2 ATR + 1 1/2 ATR + 1 + 1/2	X+3 ATR	X+2 1/2 ATR	3 1/2 ATR
8	2 ATR + 1 1/2 ATR + 1 + 1/2	X+3 1/2 ATR	X+2 1/2 ATR	4 ATR
9	2 ATR + 1 1/2 ATR + 1 + 1/2	X+4 ATR	X+2 1/2 ATR	4 1/2 ATR
10	2 ATR + 1 1/2 ATR + 1 + 1/2	X+4 1/2 ATR	X+2 1/2 ATR	5 ATR

To understand this chart, assume the following:
X = $100.
1 ATR = $4.
1 Unit = 2 ATR (2 percent of total account value)

The 2nd column (risk exposure, in ATR) should be explained further - turtles

do not count profits into exposed risk. So the 1/2 ATR profit (column 5) on unit two

accumulation level (that was the requirement to advance from the first unit to the second unit) is

not counted hence the 2 ATR +1 1/2 ATR as exposed risk.

The formula is as follows: the second unit would be 4 ATR (2 ATR + 2 ATR) as amount risked and purchased minus 1/2 ATR that was gained as profit. The second unit purchased would be 1 1/2 ATR. Stops are moved up to break even level, continuing in this fashion all the way to the 6th level. From the seventh level, we risk 1/2 ATR up to the tenth level, which would total a 5 ATR exposure.

(1/2 ATR + 1 ATR + 1 1/2 ATR + 2 ATR) = 5 ATR. Turtles never risk more than 5ATR or $50,000, whichever is larger. This is the practice called trailing stops. Although this may at first seem overly rigorous, if you don't use such calculations, the whole process becomes arbitrary, undisciplined, and believe me DANGEROUS! Reread this section if you need to, until it becomes second nature. Turtles think this way!

Stop Rules

- Once entered in a position, use a 1/2 ATR stop. If stopped out intraday, re-establish the position if a new entry signal is given (new low or high).

- The day after entry, use a 2% hard stop for protection. After the first unit, you can use a 2 ATR stop.

Trend Traders are taught to keep wide stops, moving up stops gradually as new units are added. The stop level in the chart is not the original stop before further units were added.

- The system builds up profitable positions by 1/2 ATR increases.

- When the position has 1/2 ATR gain, it allows addition of one unit (remember, one unit can be multiple contracts or just one, depending on volatility and funds at hand).

If we use an example of $100/unit price, 1 ATR is $4. You own 10 units at the end.

After buying the first unit at $100, the original stop (before any price move confirmation) is placed at $92, since the 2 ATR stop is valued at $8. Following your own set of rules (adding at 1/2 ATR increments), the second unit will be added at $102. At this point, you must move the stop from the first unit (at $92 to $94). This gradual move of stops is very important. At this time, we have two units, and both have stops at $94. The process is repeated for the first five units.

- One additional rule exists - the stops must never be moved beyond initiation price. Notice, the stop on the first unit will reach $100 when we purchase the fifth unit and stay there. When we reach the final tenth unit, the chart's limit is reached.

This generates two important safeguards: your stops are wide enough that small down drifts in price will not shake you out of building a position; yet the first five units will have a break-even stop.

Entry and Exit Signals

This system, of course, allows pyramiding, as we've seen, as an essential element; however, the method used to identify the trend may be the least important. The original developers of this system divided their funds into two portions and traded different entry/exit methods. A 20-day breakout is a very popular trend identifying method. We wish to replace the signals with Livermore's **more accurate timing** than the crude breakout that often is false unless economic conditions set us back to the high inflation times of the 70's.

For example, if prices trade in a narrow range for 19 days; on the 20th day, a lower low (or higher high) is observed. You then make your entry and take a position. Exit only if the market makes its lowest low (or highest high) of the past 6 days, in the opposite direction against the position initially taken (long or short). This may or may not work anymore.

Primary Entry rules (basically Turtle)

- Enter positions when natural reaction or secondary reaction turns into a real trend.
- Before reversing the trend, there must be a losing trade in the opposite direction.

Secondary Entry rules (basically Turtle)

- Avoid entry if the contract trades within 10 ATR of its lifetime high.
- Avoid entry if the historic ATR is 2 times the current ATR.
- Do not use trailing stops when profitable

The hardest part is maintaining discipline to keep stops wide and be willing to give back profits in the process. I must emphasize this - in a strong trend, the system's genius is that stops are kept where you, as a novice Turtle, might not expect them to be. In practice, large profits would not be entirely given back, as other liquidation signals would kick in first.

Liquidation rules (basically Turtle)

- ATR stop is triggered.

- 10 or 20 days against the position. Depends on system in use.

- Different trade is available but there is no adequate equity. In this case, liquidate the trade with largest loss or smallest gain.

- As with entry, you should scale in, and on exits you should scale-out. When the position is suffering a number of days against it, don't wait for the pre-set rule - i.e., 20 days against the position, to liquidate the whole position. Instead, liquidate 1/3 of position at 10 days against, 1/3, at 15 days against and the final 1/3 at 20 days against.

- Regardless of profit or loss - if volatility doubles from the time of initiation, get out! Don't let volatility whipsaw your position.

Final Words on the Unit Trend System

Catching a great trend is not so simple as one might assume. In the original Turtle system, very little was said about 'fake break-outs' and trend-less periods. UTS tends to handle these a bit better, with stricter rules for trend identification. Without inflation on the horizon, futures will tend to have trend-less, sideways markets. High-volume breakout, coupled with price breakout, AND open-interest increases can help establish a true trending market.

III. Summary (basic Turtle rules)

These rules were quoted by Russell Sands, one of the original Turtles, from Christopher Tate's Article . They correspond almost verbatim to my original research on this subject. I decided to use this as a reference and validation to my own rules. In addition, it is a nice summary of my turtle-trading chapter above.

Entry Rules

1. Get in on a 20-bar breakout (a bar on a bar chart = one day high (open) to low (close) represented by a bar and the close as a notch. So 1 bar = 1 day).

2. Before reversing the trend using the 20-bar breakout (20-day moving average breakout), there must be a losing trade in the opposite direction.

3. Always enter on a 55 bar breakout.

4. (Subjective) If the market is sideways, use a 55 bar breakout.

5. Once there is a profit in one direction, you can continue to trade in that direction, but to trade in the opposite direction, there must first be a loss.

Stop Rules

1. On the day of entry, use a 1/2 (Average True Range) ATR stop. If the trade gets stopped out during intraday trading, then get back in if the intraday market gives a new signal (makes new lows or highs).

2. Use a 10-day trailing stop (meaning, if you are above the 10-day moving average, get long; if below it, get short).

3. The day after the entry - use a 2 ATR protective stop. Sometimes the 10 day trailing stop is too far away. The 10-day trailing stop assures you will not be risking more than 2-ATR on a trade (except when there is a gap open against your trade).

4. When the trade is at a 2.5 ATR profit, move the protective stop to break-even.

5. Once the 10-day trailing stop or the 2.5 ATR rule moves the stop to break-even, start using a wider trailing stop of 20 bars.

6. Once you are ahead by 10 ATR, use a 3 bar pivot as a trailing stop and the 20 bar breakout as a trailing stop (The pivot stop is based on identified support and resistance levels created by actual market action. A long pivot stop would be trailed up as new support pivots are created by market action. A short pivot stop is trailed down as the market creates new resistance pivots. Successful traders use support and resistance levels in many ways. Using support and resistance levels, as stop loss points is a logical use of the support and resistance levels concept).

Additional Entry Rules

1. Enter additional positions when natural reaction or secondary reaction turns into a real trend, provided the protective stop on the first positions has been moved to break even.

2. After a big profit of 10 ATR or more, do not trade in the opposite direction.

3. Wait for a sideways market to start trading and get in on reversal if it happens.

Money Management Rules

1. Do not risk more than 1% of your account per trade.

2. Do not expose your account to more than a 2 ATR risk at any time.

3. Use fractional entry technique.

4. Wait for a trade to be moved to break even before adding any new trades.

5. Trade the strongest commodity within a complex, such as grains and currencies.

6. Trade when the volatility shrinks. When the volatility shrinks by 50%, it allows more contracts to be used for the same dollar risk.

IV. Diversification

Many who are novices to trend trading perceive the strength of this system is the pyramiding and money management. This is not quite so. The most important advantage of the trend trading system is the allowance of proper diversification. With units calculated across different contracts, the trader can always maintain a proper risk parameter even if volatility changes overnight. Ideally, Trend Trading should be used in a portfolio of commodities. The following tables (portfolio tables below) will show you what I mean.

Turtles make most of their money in 30 percent of their trades. That's why diversification is important. For example, when we may not have a meaningful trend in the stock market, oil can develop a major bull trend, or currencies can be trending very nicely, thank you. Therefore, Turtles don't just watch one market, they watch any trend in all markets. They take many small losses of 1-2% but take geometric gains when they catch a big trend and pyramid it correctly.

Portfolio Considerations

The rules regarding portfolio management are as follows: the system allows 10-unit exposure at any given time. However, there should be consideration given to circumstances when we are in 10 unit long position and there is an offsetting short position. The following tables compare two hypothetical portfolios.

Portfolio A - Lower risk

Long positions (units)	Short positions (units)
Gold (3)	Copper (3)
Silver (2)	Platinum (1)

Portfolio B - Higher risk

Long positions (units)	Short positions (units)
Gold (3)	-
Silver (2)	-

Portfolio C - Lowest risk

Long positions (units)	Short positions (units)
Gold (3)	SP 500(3)
Silver (2)	-

Here is the code for the Turtle System
(different from the one on the CD, KBTURTLE.ELS)

/// Turtle 20-Day Breakout Replica //

```
vars: N(0),StopLoss(1),DV(0),BB(0),AccountBalance(0),DollarRisk(0),LTT(0),
Tracker(0),LastTrade(0),HBP(0),LBP(0); input: InitialBalance(100000),Length(20);

if marketposition = 0 then begin
BB = 0;
N = xAverage( TrueRange, Length );
DV = N * BigPointValue;

AccountBalance = InitialBalance;
DollarRisk = AccountBalance * .01;
LTT = IntPortion(DollarRisk/DV);
StopLoss = 2 * DV * LTT;

if LastTrade = -1 then begin
buy LTT shares next bar highest(h,20) or higher;
buy LTT shares next bar highest(h,20) + (0.5*N) or higher;
buy LTT shares next bar highest(h,20) + (1.0*N) or higher;
buy LTT shares next bar highest(h,20) + (1.5*N) or higher;
sellshort LTT shares next bar lowest(l,20) or lower;
sellshort LTT shares next bar lowest(l,20) - (0.5*N) or lower;
sellshort LTT shares next bar lowest(l,20) - (1.0*N) or lower;
sellshort LTT shares next bar lowest(l,20) - (1.5*N) or lower;
end;

if LastTrade = 1 then begin
buy LTT shares next bar highest(h,55) or higher;
buy LTT shares next bar highest(h,55) + (0.5*N) or higher;
buy LTT shares next bar highest(h,55) + (1.0*N) or higher;
buy LTT shares next bar highest(h,55) + (1.5*N) or higher;
sellshort LTT shares next bar lowest(l,55) or lower;
sellshort LTT shares next bar lowest(l,55) - (0.5*N) or lower;
sellshort LTT shares next bar lowest(l,55) - (1.0*N) or lower;
sellshort LTT shares next bar lowest(l,55) - (1.5*N) or lower;
end;

end;

// PREVIOUS TRADE TRACKER
if HBP = 0 and h > highest(h,19)[1] then begin
Tracker = 1; HBP = h; LBP = 0;
end;
```

```
if LBP = 0 and l < lowest(l,19)[1] then begin
Tracker = -1; LBP = l; HBP = 0;
end;

if Tracker = 1 then begin
if l < HBP - (2*N) then LastTrade = -1;
if h > HBP + (4*N) then LastTrade = 1;
end;

if Tracker = -1 then begin
if h > LBP + (2*N) then LastTrade = -1;
if l < LBP - (4*N) then LastTrade = 1;
end;

// LONG 20
if LastTrade = -1 and marketposition = 1 then begin
BB = BB + 1;
if currentshares = LTT then begin
buy LTT shares next bar highest(h,20)[BB] + (0.5*N) or higher;
buy LTT shares next bar highest(h,20)[BB] + (1.0*N) or higher;
buy LTT shares next bar highest(h,20)[BB]+ (1.5*N) or higher;
end;

if currentshares = LTT * 2 then begin
buy LTT shares next bar highest(h,20)[BB] + (1.0*N) or higher;
buy LTT shares next bar highest(h,20)[BB] + (1.5*N) or higher;
end;

if currentshares = LTT * 3 then
buy LTT shares next bar highest(h,20)[BB] + (1.5*N) or higher;
end;

// LONG 55
if LastTrade = 1 and marketposition = 1 then begin
BB = BB + 1;
if currentshares = LTT then begin
buy LTT shares next bar highest(h,55)[BB] + (0.5*N) or higher;
buy LTT shares next bar highest(h,55)[BB] + (1.0*N) or higher;
buy LTT shares next bar highest(h,55)[BB]+ (1.5*N) or higher;
end;
if currentshares = LTT * 2 then begin
buy LTT shares next bar highest(h,55)[BB] + (1.0*N) or higher;
buy LTT shares next bar highest(h,55)[BB] + (1.5*N) or higher;
end;
if currentshares = LTT * 3 then
buy LTT shares next bar highest(h,55)[BB] + (1.5*N) or higher;
end;
sell ("out-S") next bar lowest(l,10) or lower;
```

```
// SHORT 20
if LastTrade = -1 and marketposition = -1 then begin
BB = BB + 1;
if currentshares = LTT then begin
sellshort LTT shares next bar lowest(l,20)[BB] - (0.5*N) or lower;
sellshort LTT shares next bar lowest(l,20)[BB] - (1.0*N) or lower;
sellshort LTT shares next bar lowest(l,20)[BB] - (1.5*N) or lower;
end;
if currentshares = LTT * 2 then begin
sellshort LTT shares next bar lowest(l,20)[BB] - (1.0*N) or lower;
sellshort LTT shares next bar lowest(l,20)[BB] - (1.5*N) or lower;
end;
if currentshares = LTT * 3 then
sellshort LTT shares next bar lowest(l,20)[BB] - (1.5*N) or lower;
end;

// SHORT 55
if LastTrade = 1 and marketposition = -1 then begin
BB = BB + 1;
if currentshares = LTT then begin
sellshort LTT shares next bar lowest(l,55)[BB] - (0.5*N) or lower;
sellshort LTT shares next bar lowest(l,55)[BB] - (1.0*N) or lower;
sellshort LTT shares next bar lowest(l,55)[BB] - (1.5*N) or lower;
end;
if currentshares = LTT * 2 then begin
sellshort LTT shares next bar lowest(l,55)[BB] - (1.0*N) or lower;
sellshort LTT shares next bar lowest(l,55)[BB] - (1.5*N) or lower;
end;
if currentshares = LTT * 3 then
sellshort LTT shares next bar lowest(l,55)[BB] - (1.5*N) or lower;
end;
buytocover ("out-B") next bar highest(h,10) or higher;

// STOPS
if currentshares = (2 * LTT) then StopLoss = DV * 3.5 * LTT;
if currentshares = (3 * LTT) then StopLoss = DV * 4.5 * LTT;
if currentshares = (4 * LTT) then StopLoss = DV * 5.0 * LTT;
setstoploss (StopLoss);

// COMMENTARY
commentary ("LTT: ",LTT,Newline);
commentary ("CurrentShares: ",CurrentShares,Newline);
commentary ("StopLoss: ",StopLoss,Newline);
commentary ("AccountBalance:",AccountBalance,NewLine);
commentary ("LastTrade: ",LastTrade,NewLine);
```

Appendix A

My testing revealed that S&P 500 Futures works (tests) with fixed percentage and 10-percent threshold with a modest profit.

For Stocks I used the standard 6 points and yielded a profit.

You can run optimization studies for TS 2000I and Wealth-lab developer however these studies did not yield a revelation that I had hoped.

The key is a more sophisticated money management and filtering system using the core provided hereon.

During the period from May 5th to May 21st no prices were recorded because no prices were made lower than the last price recorded the Natural Reaction column, and no sufficient rally was to be recorded.

On May 27th, the price of Bethlehem Steel was recorded in red because it was a lower price than the previous price recorded in the Downward Trend column. (See Rule 6c)

On June 10th, a price was recorded in the Secondary Rally column of Bethlehem Steel (See Rule 6e)

Due to technical difficulties this book is available only as black and white. However a Color PDF version is included in the CD-ROM for easier use.

The CD-ROM with this book is a virtual one - download for free and burn it at home.

http://spread-traders.com/PivotSwingSystem.zip

Bibliography

G. H. Kramer
Ideas in this book were used from G. H. Kramer's interpretation of the Livermore system and his programming in into TradeStation 2000i. (TradeStationWorld)

Richard Smitten
Jesse Livermore – World Greatest Stock Trader (Wiley)

Ari Kiev
Kiev –Trading To Win

Jesse Livermore
Jesse Livermore – How to Trade in Stocks (The Livermore Market Key System) – 1940 (out of print)

Edwin Lefevre
Lefevre - Reminiscences of a Stock Operator

For more information and books you can contact us at;

http://www.andras-nagy.com

Printed in the United States
75778LV00002B/469-472